hugo

in **3** MONTHS

SPANISH

Isabel Cisneros

A DORLING KINDERSLEY BOOK

LONDON, NEW YORK, MUNICH,
MELBOURNE, AND DELHI

This edition first published in Great Britain
in 2003 by Dorling Kindersley Limited,
80 Strand, London WC2R 0RL

First published in Great Britain by
Hugo's Language Books Limited

Copyright © 2003 Dorling Kindersley Limited
A Penguin Company
2 4 6 8 10 9 7 5 3

A CIP catalogue record is available from the British Library.
ISBN-13: 978-1-4053-0105-3
ISBN-10: 1 40530 105 8

Hugo Spanish in Three Months is also available in
a pack with three CDs, ISBN-13: 978-0-7513-6990-8
ISBN-10: 0 75136 990 X

Written by
Isabel Cisneros
Formerly Head of Spanish at
The Henley College

Printed and bound in China by Leo Paper Product LTD

see our complete catalogue at
www.dk.com

Preface

This updated and enlarged edition of *Hugo Spanish in Three Months* has been written by Isabel Cisneros, who has considerable experience in teaching her native tongue to sixth forms, adult beginners, and more advanced students. The book is designed for people working without a teacher, who want to acquire a good working knowledge of Spanish in a short time. The grammar is presented concisely and clearly, maintaining the Hugo principle of teaching only what is really essential – and yet providing a complete course in written and conversational Spanish. If you are using this book together with the related CDs they will give a further dimension to your studies.

Ideally you should spend about an hour a day on the course (maybe a little less if you don't use the recordings), although there is no hard and fast rule on this. Do as much as you feel capable of doing; if you have no special aptitude for language-learning, there is no point in forcing yourself beyond your daily capacity to assimilate new material. It is much better to learn a little at a time, and to learn that thoroughly.

First read each rule or numbered section carefully and re-read it to ensure that you have fully understood the grammar and examples given. Listen to the appropriate section of the CD, where you will hear most of the examples and vocabulary pronounced. Try to understand rather than memorize; if you have understood, the exercises and drills will ensure that you remember the rules through applying them. Translate the exercises and check your answers against the key at the back of the book; the vocabularies in each chapter list those words not previously supplied elsewhere in the text. If you make mistakes and cannot understand why, go back to the relevant grammar section and read it again.

Having completed the written exercises, move on to the drills and speak both stimulus and response out aloud. Work through them line by line and use them as a test to see if you are ready to move on to the next chapter.

In addition to the valuable oral practice in pronunciation and general fluency provided by these drills, they may also be treated as written exercises – answers are at the back of the book.

Each week of the course finishes with a conversation in everyday Spanish, against which you will find an English translation. It is important to remember that idiomatic language cannot be translated word for word without the occasional appearance of some rather stilted phrases. These conversations should be read aloud until you can do so without hesitation; take careful note of the use of idioms and new vocabulary, as well as relating the constructions you hear to those you have just learnt.

The course is rounded off with a selection of reading passages taken from modern Spanish literature, which you should read and read again as soon as you feel able to do so without too much need to refer to the English translations. These will add to your comprehension of the written language, and will also give you a taste of the pleasures in store, should you decide to take your study of Spanish to a more advanced level.

We hope you will enjoy *Hugo Spanish in Three Months*, and wish you success with your studies. When the course is completed, you should have a very good understanding of the language – more than sufficient for general holiday or business purposes, and enough to lead quickly into an examination syllabus if this is your eventual aim.

Contents

Pronunciation

Before you start the course, read the following rules and advice on pronunciation. There's no need to learn these rules by heart; refer back to them at frequent intervals and you will soon know them well. If you use our recordings, everything will be made much clearer; these CDs enable you to hear the Spanish words and phrases at the same time as you read them. As Spanish is a very phonetic language, once you are familiar with its sounds you will always know how to pronounce the printed word.

STRESS
In Spanish, the following rules apply:

1 Most words ending in a vowel, **n** or **s**, bear the stress on the next to last syllable:
examen, flores, hombre, cigarrillo.

2 Most words ending in a consonant other than **n** or **s**, bear the stress on the last syllable:
papel, ciudad, mujer, capital.

3 Exceptions to these two rules are indicated by a written accent on the stressed syllable:
árbol, lámpara, estación, inglés, música.

4 The written accent is also used to distinguish words which have the same spelling but different meanings:
el (the), **él** (he); **si** (if), **sí** (yes); **mi** (my), **mí** (me); **mas** (but), **más** (more).

5 The vowels **a**, **e**, and **o** are strong vowels; **i** and **u** are weak ones. When two strong vowels come together, they are pronounced separately:
paella, teatro, poeta.

When two weak vowels come together, the stress is on the last one:
cuida, viuda.

When a strong vowel and a weak one come together, the

strong vowel is stressed unless the weak one is accentuated: *a*ire, j*a*ula, oído, aún.

In our 'imitated pronunciation' (see page 12) we show which is the stressed syllable by marking ' in front of it.

PRONUNCIATION OF VOWELS

The Spanish vowels are **a**, **e**, **i**, **o**, and **u**. Each vowel has only one sound; this is not quite so long and broad as the English equivalent given below. The vowel sounds are also shortened, as in other languages, when they occur in an unstressed word or syllable, or preceding a consonant.

a   is pronounced like 'ah' in English:
        al (to), **la** (the), **casa** (house).

e   is pronounced like 'ay':
        me (me), **de** (from), **le** (him).

i   is pronounced like 'ee':
        mi (my), **prima** (cousin).

o   is pronounced like 'o':
        lo (the), **no** (no), **gato** (cat).

u   is pronounced like 'oo':
        tu (your), **su** (their), **uno** (one).

PRONUNCIATION OF CONSONANTS

There are only two Spanish consonants that are pronounced quite unlike their English counterparts: **z** and **j**. There are others which differ in various lesser ways. Note the following points:

z   is pronounced like 'th' in 'month' or 'thick':
        voz, luz, paz, vez, zapato.

j   is pronounced like the German guttural 'ch' as in 'auch', or like 'ch' in the Scottish 'loch'. This sound is merely the English h pronounced in the throat: if you find it hard to

make, simply pronounce it like an aspirated h:
ojo, jugar, juzgar, caja.

ch   is pronounced as in 'cheap' or 'much':
muchacha.

c   before **e** or **i** is pronounced like the Spanish **z**:
cena, cinco, once.

g   before **e** or **i** is pronounced like the Spanish **j**:
coger, general, gigante.

g   before any other letter is like g in 'go':
gato.

gu   before **e** or **i** is like g in 'go'; before any other vowel it
is like 'gw-' or 'goo':
guerra, guía.

h   is not pronounced at all:
hijo, hablar.

ll   is pronounced nearly like 'll' in 'million':
calle, silla, llamar.

ñ   is almost like 'ni' in 'companion':
niño, señor.

qu   is like English k:
que, quince.

r   is rolled on the tip of the tongue more than in English,
especially at the beginning of a word or syllable: **raro.**

s   is always pronounced sharp, as in 'see' or 'last', never
like an English z sound as in 'easy' or 'miser':
casa, mesa.

y   is like y in 'yes': **yo**. But alone or at the end of a word
it is like the Spanish vowel **i** ('ee'):
y, soy.

VARYING PRONUNCIATIONS

The lisping pronunciation of **z**, and of **c** before **e** or **i**, is usual in Castile; as Castilian is considered the best Spanish, we recommend that you adopt this pronunciation in preference to any other variations you may hear. But in Central and South America (and in some parts of Spain) it is usual to pronounce **z**, and **c** before **e** or **i**, like the English s.

Many Spaniards pronounce the final **d** like 'th' in 'thin', 'myth'; some will pronounce **d** in the middle of a word like 'th' in 'then'. This you should avoid copying; remember to pronounce **madre** as ['mah-dray], not as ['mah-thray]. A final **d** should not be made too sharp or distinct.

It is also not unusual for Spaniards to confuse the sound of **b** with that of **v**, so that **vaca** sounds like 'baca', for example. This is not wrong, and the CD recordings of this course will illustrate it throughout – see note in section 18.

The letter **ll** is pronounced in several ways; we imitate it as [l'y], but in some areas of Spain and in Latin America it has a strong guttural sound, with the 'l' virtually disappearing. In the Spanish province of Andalusia and in Argentina it is even stronger, the 'l' sound being replaced by something like a soft j or the 'si' in 'occasion'. Thus **mantilla**, which we imitate as [mahn-'tee-l'yah], becomes [mahn-'tee-yah] or [mahn-'tee-j'yah].

PUNCTUATION SIGNS AND ACCENTS

Question marks and exclamation marks are placed at both ends of the phrase, the first one being inverted. The diaeresis (¨) is placed over **u** when preceded by **g**, to show that the **u** must be pronounced: **agüero**. The tilde (~) is placed over **n**, when that letter is to be pronounced like 'ni' in 'onion': **mañana**. The use of the acute accent (´) in Spanish is explained on page 7. It never alters the pronunciation of a letter. It is also used in such words as **cuándo** and **dónde** (when, where), when they actually ask a question: **¿Cuándo llega el buque?** (When does the boat arrive?) but **Me alegre cuando llega el buque** (I am glad when the boat arrives).

THE SPANISH ALPHABET

This consists of 29 letters, of which **K** and **W** are found only in words taken from other languages. Note the letters **CH**, **LL**, and **Ñ**. In Spanish dictionaries, words beginning with any one of these will be found listed separately – for example, you will not find a word beginning with **CH** by looking under **C**. These letters occur in dictionaries in the order shown below, with **CH** coming after **C**, **LL** after **L**, and **Ñ** after **N**. Below, we give the 'name' of each letter written according to our system of imitated pronunciation (explained below).

A	(ah)
B	(bay)
C	(thay)
CH	(chay)
D	(day)
E	(ay)
F	('eff-ay)
G	(Hay)
H	('ah-chay)
I	(ee)
J	('Ho-tah)
K	(kah)
L	('ell-ay)
LL	('ell-yay)
M	('emm-ay)
N	('enn-ay)
Ñ	('enn-yay)
O	(o)
P	(pay)
Q	(koo)
R	('airr-ay)
S	('ess-ay)
T	(tay)
U	(oo)
V	('oo-vay)
W	('oo-vay-'do-blay)
X	('ay-kiss)
Y	(ee-gre-'ay-gah)
Z	('thay-tah)

THE 'IMITATED PRONUNCIATION'

For the first four weeks we give the imitated pronunciation of each new word, in footnotes to the section or vocabulary list in which they first appear. In this imitated pronunciation the Spanish sounds are represented by English syllables; read it as if each syllable were part of an English word and you should always be understood, more especially if you bear in mind the modifications noted below. When reading the imitated pronunciation, remember that:

th   (printed bold face) must be pronounced like 'th' in 'thin', never as in 'they'.

H   (printed as a capital) is to be pronounced gutturally, like 'ch' in the Scottish 'loch' (not 'lock').

s   is always like 'ss' in 'missing', never like 's' in 'easy'.

ah   represents the Spanish **a**; this sounds like 'ah', but it is shorter than in 'harm', 'cast'. It is never like the 'a' in 'hat', but remember to keep it short and sharp.

o   resembles the sound of 'o' in 'not', and even slightly approaches the 'aw' in 'law'. It is not as long as in 'go'.

Week 1

- *how to say 'the', 'a', and 'some'*
- *how to recognize whether a noun is masculine or feminine, and which article to use with each gender*
- *formation of the plural*
- *how to say 'I', 'you', 'he', 'she', 'it', 'we', 'they'*
- *forms of address: Mr., Mrs., etc*
- *formation of the negative and interrogative*
- *the present tense of 'tener', 'to have'*

1 ARTICLES: THE, A, AN, SOME

Articles ('the', 'a', etc) agree in gender and number with the noun to which they relate. Thus, if the noun is masculine and singular, the preceding article must also be masculine singular (indicated by 'm.s.' in the paragraphs below, with similar abbreviations for feminine and plural). The definite article 'the' is expressed by:

el (m.s.)	**el libro**	the book
la (f.s.)	**la casa**	the house
los (m.pl.)	**los libros**	the books
las (f.pl.)	**las casas**	the houses

The indefinite article 'a', 'an', 'some' is expressed by:

un (m.s.)	**un libro**	a book
una (f.s.)	**una casa**	a house
unos (m.pl.)	**unos libros**	(some) books
unas (f.pl.)	**unas casas**	(some) houses

NOTE: The masculine article is used before a feminine singular noun beginning with **a** or **ha**, if the **a** or **ha** takes the stress:

el agua water
el hambre hunger

IMITATED PRONUNCIATION (1)

ell 'lee-bro; lah 'kah-sah; los lee-bros; lahs 'kah-sahs; oon 'lee-bro; 'oo-nah 'kah-sah; 'oo-nos 'lee-bros; 'oo-nahs 'kah-sahs; ell 'ah-goo'ah; ell 'ahm-bray.

2 GENDER OF NOUNS

All nouns are either masculine or feminine. There are no neuter nouns. Most nouns ending in **o** are masculine. Most nouns ending in **a**, **ión**, **d**, **z** are feminine. There are exceptions however:

la mano (f.) hand
el camión (m.) lorry
el lápiz (m.) pencil
el guardia (m.) policeman

Several words ending in **a** (of Greek origin) are masculine:

el idioma language
el mapa map

Nouns ending in other letters are of varying genders:

el hombre man
la mujer woman
la leche milk
el color colour

IMITATED PRONUNCIATION (2)

lah 'mah-no; ell kah-me-'on; ell 'lah-pi**th**;
ell goo''ah-de-ah; ell e-de-'o-mah; ell 'mah-pah;
ell 'om-bray; lah moo-'Hairr; lah 'lay-chay; ell ko-'lorr.

3 | PLURAL OF NOUNS

The plural of nouns is formed by adding **s** to nouns ending in a vowel, and **es** to nouns ending in a consonant:

hombre (man)→ **hombres** (men)
mujer (woman)→ **mujeres** (women)

The plural of nouns ending in **z** is formed by changing the **z** into **c** and adding **es**:

lápiz (pencil)→ **lápices** (pencils)
luz (light)→ **luces** (lights)

Nouns ending in a consonant and bearing an accent on the last syllable lose that accent when the plural is formed:

camión (lorry)→ **camiones** (lorries)

IMITATED PRONUNCIATION (3)

'om-bracc; moo-'Hairr-ace; 'lah-pith-ace; looth; 'looth-ace; kah-me-'on-ace.

Exercise 1

Form the plural of:

1	El libro (book)	**7**	El jardín (garden)
2	La casa (house)	**8**	El coche (car)
3	La mujer (woman)	**9**	La capital (capital)
4	El hombre (man)	**10**	La ciudad (city, town)
5	La calle (street)	**11**	La luz (light)
6	La flor (flower)	**12**	La ley (law)

IMITATED PRONUNCIATION (EX. 1)

5 'kah-l'yay; 6 florr; 7 Harr-'deen; 8 'ko-chay;
9 kah-pe-'tahl; 10 the'oo-'dahd; 12 'lay'e.

Exercise 2

Put the appropriate definite article before the following nouns:

1 ... libros (m., books)
2 ... vino (m., wine)
3 ... mesas (f., tables)
4 ... cerveza (f., beer)
5 ... pez (m., fish)
6 ... árboles (m., trees)
7 ... padre (m., father)
8 ... madre (f., mother)
9 ... lápiz (m., pencil)
10 ... estaciones (f., stations)
11 ... billete (m., ticket)
12 ... tren (m., train)

Repeat the above exercise using the indefinite article.

IMITATED PRONUNCIATION

'vee-no; 'may-sahs; **th**airr-'vay-**th**ah; pe**th**; 'arr-bol-ace; 'pah-dray; 'mah-dray; 'lah-pi**th**; ess-tah-the-'on-ace; be-l''yay-tay; trren.

Exercise 3

Translate:

1	the book	7	a city
2	the table	8	some lights
3	the tickets	9	the garden
4	some trees	10	a street
5	a beer	11	some women
6	the car	12	the station

4 SUBJECT PRONOUNS: I, YOU, HE, ETC

yo	I
tú	you (fam.)
él, ella	he, she
usted	you (pol.)

plural

nosotros (m.), nosotras (f.)	we
vosotros (m.), vosotras (f.)	you (fam.)
ellos (m.), ellas (f.)	they
ustedes	you (pol.)

The forms **tú** and **vosotros/as** (familiar forms) are used to address members of the family, friends, children and animals. The forms **usted** and **ustedes** (polite forms) are used to address all other people; usually written as **Vd.** and **Vds.**, or **Ud./Uds.**, they must always be used with the third person of the verb. **Usted** is a contraction of the archaic form of address **Vuestra Merced**, 'your honour'. Although the familiar form is becoming increasingly common in Spain, it is still advisable to use the polite form when addressing strangers or people you have just met.

Except for **usted** and **ustedes** (which are nearly always expressed), all other subject pronouns are omitted unless emphasis is required or ambiguity must be avoided.

IMITATED PRONUNCIATION (4)

yo; too; ell; 'ell-yah; oos-'ted; nos-'otros; nos-'o-trahs; vos-'o-tros; vos-'o-trahs; 'ell-yos; 'ell-yahs; oos-'tay-dace.

1

The titles **señor** (sir/Mr.), **señora** (madam/Mrs.), and **señorita** (Miss) are used to address people whose name is not known. They are also used in front of the person's surname, and **señorita** can be employed in front of the person's Christian name. These titles are always preceded by the definite article, except when they are being used to address the person directly. When used in front of a name they are usually written in abbreviated form as: **Sr., Sra., Srta**.

¿Un café, señor?	Coffee, Sir?
El Sr. Martínez.	Mr. Martínez.
La Sra. Martínez.	Mrs. Martínez.
La Srta. Martínez.	Miss Martínez.
Por aquí, Sr. Martínez.	This way, Mr. Martínez.

The titles **Don** and **Doña**, for which there are no equivalents in English, are used in front of the person's Christian name. Thus: **Don Juan; Doña María**.

IMITATED PRONUNCIATION (5)

say-n''yorr; say-n''yor-rah; say-n'yor-'ree-tah; kah-'fay; marr-'tee-ne**th**; porr ah-'kee; don Hoo''ahn; 'don-yah mah-'rree-ah.

This is an irregular verb, and one of the most important in the language, so learn it thoroughly.

present tense

tengo	I have
tienes	you have
tiene	he, she has, you have (polite form)
tenemos	we have
tenéis	you have
tienen	they have, you have (polite form)

Tienen una hija. They have a daughter.
Tenemos un coche. We have a car.

IMITATED PRONUNCIATION (6)

tay-'nairr; 'ten-go; te-'ay-nace; te-'ay-nay; tay-'nay-mos; tay-'nay-iss; te-'ay-nen; 'ee-Hah.

7 NEGATIVE FORM

The negative is formed by putting the word **no** in front of the verb:

No tengo dinero. I have no money.
No tienen cerveza. They haven't (any) beer.

8 QUESTION FORM

A sentence is made interrogative by putting the subject after the verb:

Vd. tiene una pluma. You have a pen.
¿Tiene Vd. una pluma? Have you a pen?

The interrogative is also indicated by intonation in the voice. Note that in Spanish an inverted question mark is placed at the beginning of a written question.

9 IDIOMATIC USES OF 'TENER'

There are a number of idioms with **tener** followed by a noun where English usually has 'to be' followed by an adjective. Here are some examples:

tener ... años   to be ... years old
tener calor   to be hot
tener cuidado   to be careful
tener en cuenta   to bear in mind

tener éxito	to be successful
tener frío	to be cold
tener ganas de	to feel like, to be keen on
tener gracia	to be funny
tener hambre	to be hungry
tener miedo	to be afraid
tener paciencia	to be patient
tener prisa	to be in a hurry
tener que hacer	to have things to do
tener que ver con	to have to do with
tener razón	to be right
tener sed	to be thirsty
tener sueño	to be sleepy
tener suerte	to be lucky

When **tener que** is followed by an infinitive, it translates 'to have to', 'must':

Tengo que salir. I have to go out.
Tenemos que ver la iglesia. We must see the church.

IMITATED PRONUNCIATION (9)

'ah-n'yos; kah-'lor; koo'ee-'dah-do; en koo-'en-tah;
'ex-e-to; 'free-o; 'gah-nas day; 'grah-**th**e-ah; 'ahm-bray;
mee-'ay-do; pah-**th**e-'en-**th**e-ah; 'pree-sah: kay ah-
'**th**airr; kay vairr kon; rrah-'**th**on; sayd; soo''ay-n'yo;
soo''air-tay; tay-'nairr kay; sah-'leerr; vairr; e-'glay-se-ah.

As you work through the chapters, your vocabulary will steadily be increased by the introduction of new words in the sentences that illustrate grammar explanations. Additional vocabulary lists like the one below, where fresh words are shown in the order you will come upon them in the following exercise, should be learnt before you begin the written translation work. If you find a word repeated, and you've learnt it already, don't worry!

VOCABULARY

el café	coffee
trabajar	to work
todo	everything
salir	to go out
el hijo	son

IMITATED PRONUNCIATION

kah-'fay; trah-bah-'Harr; 'to-do; sah-'leerr; 'ee-Ho.

Exercise 4

Translate:

1 They have a house.

2 We haven't (any) coffee.

3 The man is afraid.

4 I have to work.

5 Have you (fam. sing.) a pencil?

6 They are not thirsty.

7 Have you (pol. pl.) everything?

8 I am hot.

9 We have to go out.

10 He has a son.

Drill 1

In this and similar drills that follow, first read the example which shows both a 'stimulus' and a 'response' (not necessarily a simple question and answer). The model will show you how to tackle the rest of that drill. Thus, in the following you will see that the stimulus requires a response alternating between the first persons singular and plural.

Example:
¿Tiene Vd. una pluma? Have you a pen?
No, no tengo una pluma. No, I haven't a pen.
¿Tienen Vds. un lápiz? Have you (pl.) a pencil?
No, no tenemos un lápiz. No, we haven't a pencil.

1 ¿Tiene Vd. hambre?
2 ¿Tienen Vds. cerveza?
3 ¿Tiene Vd. sed?
4 ¿Tienen Vds. calor?
5 ¿Tiene Vd. frío?
6 ¿Tienen Vds. los libros?
7 ¿Tienen Vds. los billetes?

CONVERSATION A

SR. **¿Tiene Vd. una cerveza muy fría? Tengo sed.**
SRA. **Sí, señor. Aquí tiene.**
SR. **¿Cuánto es?**
SRA. **Cincuenta céntimos.**
SR. **Sólo tengo un billete de diez euros. ¿Tiene Vd. cambio?**
SRA. **Sí, señor.**
SR. **Gracias. Adiós.**

TRANSLATION A

MAN	Have you a very cold beer? I am thirsty.
WOMAN	Yes, Sir. Here you are.
MAN	How much is it?
WOMAN	Fifty centimos.
MAN	I only have a ten euro note. Have you got change?
WOMAN	Yes, Sir.
MAN	Thank you. Goodbye.

CONVERSATION B

SRA.	**Carmen y Luis tienen un piso en la ciudad y una casa en el campo.**
SR.	**¿Tiene la casa un jardín grande?**
SRA.	**Sí, muy grande y muy bonito, con árboles y flores. También tienen un perro y un gato.**

TRANSLATION B

WOMAN	Carmen and Luis have a flat in town and a house in the country.
MAN	Has the house got a large garden?
WOMAN	Yes, very big and very pretty, with trees and flowers. They also have a dog and a cat.

Week 2

- contracted forms of articles
- how to express possession ('John's father')
- some common adjectives, and how they must agree in gender and number with the noun to which they are attached
- the difference between 'ser' and 'estar', both meaning 'to be'
- how to use these important verbs

10 CONTRACTION OF ARTICLE

When the prepositions **a** (to) and **de** (of, from) are followed by the definite article **el** they contract into **al** and **del** respectively: **al castillo** (to the castle), **del jardín** (from the garden).

11 POSSESSION ('JOHN'S FATHER')

There is no possessive case in Spanish. Possession must be expressed by the preposition **de**:

El padre de Juan John's father (lit. The father of John).
El paraguas de la mujer The woman's umbrella.

IMITATED PRONUNCIATION (10/11)

ah, day; ahl kahs-'teel-l'yo; dayl Harr-'deen; 'pah-dray; pah-'rrah-goo'ahs.

Exercise 5

Translate:

1 to the church
2 of the language
3 to the car
4 to the table
5 of the trees
6 to the house
7 of the man
8 of the city
9 to the street
10 of the wine
11 to the policeman
12 of the station

Adjectives agree in gender and number with the nouns they qualify, and generally follow the noun. Adjectives ending in **o** in the masculine change the **o** to **a** in the feminine. The plural is formed by adding **s** to both genders:

El coche blanco	The white car
La casa blanca	The white house
Los coches blancos	The white cars
Las casas blancas	The white houses

Adjectives ending in **e**, and most adjectives ending in a consonant, have the same form for both masculine and feminine. The plural is formed by adding **s** to those ending in **e**, and **es** to those ending in a consonant.

For example:

El lápiz verde	The green pencil
La pared verde	The green wall
Los lápices verdes	The green pencils
Las paredes verdes	The green walls
Un ejercicio fácil	An easy exercise
Una lección fácil	An easy lesson
Unos ejercicios fáciles	Some easy exercises
Unas lecciones fáciles	Some easy lessons

Exceptions to this rule are:

1 Adjectives of nationality

inglés	English (m.)	**inglesa**	English (f.)
español	Spanish (m.)	**española**	Spanish (f.)

2 Certain adjectives ending in **n** and **or**

holgazán	lazy (m.)
holgazana	lazy (f.)
trabajador	hard-working (m.)
trabajadora	hard-working (f.)

IMITATED PRONUNCIATION (12)

'blahn-ko; 'blahn-kah; 'blahn-kos; 'blahn-kahs;
'vairr-day; pah-'re**th**; 'vairr-dace; pah-'re**th**-ace; ay-Hairr-
'**th**ee-**th**e-o; 'fah-**th**il; leck-**th**e-'on; ay-Hairr-'**th**ee-**th**e-
os; 'fah-**th**il-ace; leck-**th**e-'on-ace; in-'gless; in-'gless-ah;
es-pah-'n'yol; es-pah-'n'yo-lah; ol-gah-'**th**ahn; ol-gah-
'**th**ahn-ah; trah-bah-Hah-'dorr; trah-bah-Hah-'dor-rah.

VOCABULARY

el periódico	newspaper	**barato**	cheap
la revista	magazine	**largo**	long
interesante	interesting	**alto**	tall
encantador	charming	**alemán**	German
bueno	good	**americano**	American
útil	useful		

IMITATED PRONUNCIATION

pay-rre-'o-de-ko; rray-'viss-tah; in-tay-ress-'an-tay;
en-kahn-tah-'dorr; boo''ay-no; 'oo-til; bah-'rah-to;
'lar-go; 'ahl-to; ah-lay-'mahn; ah-mair-e-'kah-no.

Exercise 6

Make the following adjectives agree where necessary:

1 Unos hombres (bueno).
2 Una mujer (encantador).
3 Unos libros (útil).
4 Unas flores (blanco).
5 Un coche (barato).
6 Una calle (largo).
7 Unos árboles (alto).
8 Unas ciudades (interesante).
9 Un periódico (americano).
10 Una revista (alemán).

13 'SER' AND 'ESTAR'

It is important to distinguish between the verbs **ser** and **estar**, both of which translate the English 'to be'.

2

present tenses

ser	estar	to be
soy	**estoy**	I am
eres	**estás**	you are
es	**está**	he/she is, you are (pol.)
somos	**estamos**	we are
sois	**estáis**	you are
son	**están**	they are, you are (pol.)

IMITATED PRONUNCIATION (13)

sairr; es-'tahrr; soy; 'eh-ress; ess; 'so-mos; 'so'ees; son; es-'toy; es-'tahs; es-'tah; es-'tah-mos; es-'tah'ees; es-'tahn.

14 USES OF 'SER'

Ser expresses an inherent characteristic or permanent state and it is used to indicate:

1 Identity

Soy Carmen. I am Carmen.

2 Possession

El perro es de Juan. The dog is John's.

3 Origin

Mis amigos son de Madrid.
My friends are from Madrid.

4 Nationality

Somos ingleses. We are English.

5 Occupation

El padre de María es arquitecto.
Maria's father is an architect.

6 Material of which something is made

El reloj es de oro. The watch is made of gold.

7 Inherent characteristics
Carlos es muy alto. Charles is very tall.

8 Expressions of time

Son las cinco. It is five o'clock.
Hoy es lunes. Today is Monday.

9 Impersonal expressions

Es mejor esperar. It is better to wait.
Es difícil aprender. It is difficult to learn.

Ser is also used with the past participle of the verb to form the passive voice (see section 82 for further notes on the passive):

El ladrón es apresado por la policía.
The thief is captured by the police.

IMITATED PRONUNCIATION (14)

'pairr-o; mees ah-'mee-gos; mah-'dreeth; arr-ke-'teck-to;
rray-'loH; 'o-ro; moo'e; 'thin-ko; oy'e; 'loo-ness;
may-'Horr; ess-pay-'rahrr; de-'fee-**th**il; ah-pren-'dairr;
lah-'dron; ah-pray-'sah-do; po-le-'**th**ee-ah.

15 USES OF 'ESTAR'

2

Estar is used to indicate:

1 Temporary states or conditions
Pedro está enfermo. Peter is ill.

2 Position (whether temporary or permanent)

Carmen está en el salón. Carmen is in the lounge.
Valencia está en España. Valencia is in Spain.

Estar is also used with the present participle of the verb to form the continuous tenses:

Los niños están jugando en el jardín.
The children are playing in the garden.

Estar with the preposition **para** translates 'to be about to':

El tren está para llegar. The train is about to arrive.

These basic rules, however, do not cover every situation. There are cases where it is difficult for the student to decide which verb is the right one. For instance, it can be argued that to be young (**joven**) or to be rich (**rico**) is a temporary condition, but in both cases **ser** is used. In the exercise on the following page an English translation will help you decide whether each sentence is 'temporary' or 'permanent'.

IMITATED PRONUNCIATION (15)

en-'fairr-mo; sah-'lonn; vah-'len-**th**e-ah; ess-'pah-n'yah; 'nee-n'yos; Hoo-'gahn-do; 'pah-rrah; l'yay-'garr; 'Ho-ven; 'rree-ko.

Exercise 7

Write down these sentences in Spanish, with the appropriate form of 'ser' or 'estar' where we have omitted them.

1 Las lecciones ... difíciles.   The lessons are difficult.

2 El café ... frío.   The coffee is cold.

3 Las chicas ... alemanas.   The girls are German.

4 Jaime ... muy inteligente.   James is very intelligent.

5 Los libros ... sobre la mesa.   The books are on the table.

6 Ana ... triste.   Ann is sad.

7 La mujer de Luis ... secretaria.   Luis's wife is a secretary.

8 La casa ... pequeña.   The house is small.

9 El coche no ... en el garaje.   The car is not in the garage.

10 Yo ... contento con el hotel.   I am pleased with the hotel.

VOCABULARY

italiano	Italian	la colina	hill
la manzana	apple	peligroso	dangerous
en	in	fumar	to smoke
la cocina	kitchen	demasiado	too much
el autobús	bus	dulce	sweet
allí	there	mañana	tomorrow
la capital	capital	domingo	Sunday
España	Spain	la playa	beach

IMITATED PRONUNCIATION (7)

'chee-kahs; 'so-bray; 'triss-tay; say-kray-'tah-ree-ah;
pay-'kay-n'yah; gah-'rrah-Hay; con-'ten-to; con;
ee-tah-lee-'ah-no; mahn-'thah-nah; en; ko-'thee-nah;
ah'oo-to-'booss; ah-'l'yee; kah-pe-'tahl; ess-'pahn-yah;
ko-'lee-nah; pay-le-'gro-so; foo-'mahrr;
day-mah-se-'ah-do; dool-thay; mah-'n'yah-nah;
do-'meen-go; 'plah-yah.

Exercise 8

Translate:

1 She is Italian.
2 The apples are in the kitchen.
3 The bus is over there.
4 Madrid is the capital of Spain.
5 The girl is tall.
6 The house is on the hill.
7 It is dangerous to smoke.
8 The coffee is too sweet.
9 Tomorrow is Sunday.
10 They are on the beach.

CONVERSATION A

JUAN   ¿Dónde está tu padre?
TERESA   Está en el jardín, tomando el sol y leyendo el periódico.
JUAN   Y tu madre ¿dónde está?
TERESA   Está en la cocina haciendo una paella para la comida.
JUAN   ¡Una paella! ¡Qué bien!

TRANSLATION A

JUAN	Where is your father?
TERESA	He is in the garden sunbathing and reading the paper.
JUAN	And your mother, where is she?
TERESA	She is in the kitchen making a paella for lunch.
JUAN	Paella! How lovely!

CONVERSATION B

RECEPCIONISTA	**¿Es Vd. el señor García?**
SR. GARCÍA	**Sí.**
RECEPCIONISTA	**Tengo un fax para Vd.**
SR. GARCÍA	**¿De dónde es el fax?**
RECEPCIONISTA	**Es de Los Angeles.**
SR. GARCÍA	**Ah! Muchas gracias.**
RECEPCIONISTA	**De nada.**

TRANSLATION B

RECEPTIONIST	Are you Mr. García?
MR. GARCÍA	Yes.
RECEPTIONIST	I have a fax for you.
MR. GARCÍA	Where is the fax from?
RECEPTIONIST	It's from Los Angeles.
MR. GARCÍA	Oh! Thank you.
RECEPTIONIST	Not at all.

Week 3

- demonstrative adjectives and pronouns ('this', 'that', 'these', 'those')
- present tense of regular verbs ending in '-ar', '-er', '-ir'
- use of the present participle ('speaking', 'eating')
- interrogative pronouns ('what?', 'who?', 'whose?', etc)
- relative pronouns ('who', 'which', 'that', 'of whom', etc)

16 DEMONSTRATIVE ADJECTIVES: THIS, THAT, THESE, THOSE

	masculine	feminine
this	este	esta
that	ese	esa
that (over there)	aquel	aquella
these	estos	estas
those	esos	esas
those (over there)	aquellos	aquellas

Demonstrative adjectives always precede the noun and agree with it in gender and number:

Este coche	This car
Esa iglesia	That church
Aquellos niños	Those children (over there)

A demonstrative adjective cannot be used before one noun and understood (but omitted) before another. It must be repeated:

| **Estos niños y estas niñas** | These boys and girls |
| **Esas mesas y esas sillas** | Those tables and chairs |

VOCABULARY

caro	expensive
fuerte	strong
muy	very
viejo	old
el amigo	friend
ocupado	occupied, taken, busy
libre	free
el ascensor	lift, elevator
lleno	full
la uva	grape
agrio	sour

IMITATED PRONUNCIATION (16)

'es-tay; 'ay-say; ah-'kel; 'es-tos; 'ay-sos; ah-'kell-yos; 'es-tah; 'ay-sah; ah-'kell-yah; 'es-tahs; 'ay-sahs; ah-'kell-yahs; 'kah-ro; foo''air-tay; 'moo'e; ve-'ay-Ho; ah-'mee-go; o-koo-'pah-do; 'lee-bray; ahs-**th**en-'sor; 'l'yay-no; 'oo-vah; 'ah-gre-o.

Exercise 9

Translate:

1 That car is expensive.

2 Those men are strong.

3 That church is very old.

4 These friends are from Malaga.

5 This table is taken.

6 That man is free.

7 This lift is full.

8 Those grapes are sour.

9 Those books (over there) are interesting.

10 It is that beach (over there).

17 DEMONSTRATIVE PRONOUNS

These have the same forms as demonstrative adjectives but usually take an accent on the stressed syllable. They agree in gender and number with the noun they replace.

For example:

No es este libro, es aquél.
It isn't this book, it's that one over there.
Estos zapatos son caros, ésos son baratos.
These shoes are expensive, those are cheap.

The neuter forms of the pronoun **esto** (this) and **eso, aquello** (that) are used to refer to things the gender of which has not been established. These forms have no plural.

¿Qué es esto? What is this?
Eso no es correcto. That is not correct.

Éste and **aquél**, with their related forms, translate the English 'the latter' and 'the former' respectively:

Tienen un hijo y una hija. Ésta es enfermera, aquél es médico.
They have a son and daughter. The latter is a nurse, the former is a doctor.

VOCABULARY

la maleta	suitcase
la galleta	biscuit
el pan	bread
el abrigo	coat
el zapato	shoe
el vino	wine
la habitación	room

IMITATED PRONUNCIATION

mah-'lay-tah; gahl-'yay-tah; pahn; ah-'bree-go;
thah-'pah-to; 'vee-no; ah-be-tah-**th**e-'on.

Exercise 10

3

Replace the words in brackets by the correct form of
the demonstrative adjective or pronoun:

1 No son (these) libros, son (those ones).
2 No es (that) maleta, es (that one over there).
3 No son (these) galletas, son (those ones).
4 No es (that) pan, es (this one).
5 No es (this) abrigo, es (that one over there).
6 No son (those) zapatos, son (these ones).
7 No es (this) vino, es (that one).
8 No es (that) periódico, es (this one).
9 No son (these) habitaciones, son (those ones).
10 No es (this) coche, es (that one over there).

18 REGULAR VERBS

The infinitive of every Spanish verb ends in **ar**, **er**, or **ir**
(**hablar**, **comer**, **vivir**). The part preceding these endings
is called the stem. Most tenses are formed by adding
certain personal endings to the stem. These endings are
shown below:

present tenses

hablar	comer	vivir
to speak	to eat	to live
habl/o	com/o	viv/o
habl/as	com/es	viv/es
habl/a	com/e	viv/e
habl/amos	com/emos	viv/imos
habl/áis	com/éis	viv/ís
habl/an	com/en	viv/en

No hablo ruso.	I don't speak Russian.
¿Habla Vd. español?	Do you speak Spanish?
Come mucho pan.	He eats a lot of bread.
No comen en el hotel.	They don't eat in the hotel.
¿Viven Vds. aquí?	Do you live here?
Vivo en Londres.	I live in London.

3

VOCABULARY

comprar	to buy
beber	to drink
escribir	to write
estudiar	to study
aprender	to learn
subir	to go up, to bring up

IMITATED PRONUNCIATION (18)

ah-'blahrr; 'ah-blo; 'ah-blahs; 'ah-blah; ah-'blah-mos;
ah-'blah-ees; 'ah-blahn; ko-'mairr; 'ko-mo; 'ko-mes;
'ko-may; ko-'may-mos; ko-'may-ees; 'ko-men; ve-'veerr;
'vee-vo; 'vee-ves; 'vee-vay; ve-'vee-mos; ve-'vees;
'vee-ven; 'rroo-so; 'moo-cho; 'lon-dress; kom-'prahrr;
bay-'bairr; ess-kre-'beerr; ess-too-de-'ahrr;
ah-pren-'dairr; soo-'beerr.

In listening to the recording of **vivir** in particular,
students will have noticed the tendency towards
pronouncing **v** as **b**. This is what you'll hear more often
than not in Spain, and – as we have pointed out in the
introductory paragraph dealing with varying
pronunciations on page 10 – it is quite acceptable and not
incorrect. However, throughout the printed text we have
imitated the Spanish **v** with an English v.

Exercise 11

Translate:

1 I buy.
2 He smokes.
3 You (pol.s.) drink.
4 We write.
5 They learn.
6 I study.
7 You (fam.s.) speak.
8 She eats.
9 We live.
10 They go up.
11 I learn.
12 He drinks.

Exercise 12

Translate:

1 He buys a newspaper.
2 Does she drink beer?
3 Pedro lives in Barcelona.
4 I write to Conchita.
5 Do you study English?
6 These children learn Spanish.
7 He eats too much.
8 We go up the hill.
9 I speak English.
10 They drink cheap wine.

PRESENT PARTICIPLE ('SPEAKING', 'EATING')

The present participle of regular verbs is formed by adding **-ando** to the stem of verbs in **ar**, and **-iendo** to the stem of verbs in **er** and **ir**.

For example:
hablar→ **hablando** (speaking)
comer→ **comiendo** (eating)
vivir→ **viviendo** (living)

3

The present participle used with the present tense of the verb **estar** forms the present continuous tense ('I am speaking', 'I am eating', 'I am living', etc):

present continuous
hablar (to speak)   **comer** (to eat)   **vivir** (to live)

estoy hablando	estoy comiendo	estoy viviendo
estás hablando	estás comiendo	estás viviendo
está hablando	está comiendo	está viviendo
estamos hablando	estamos comiendo	estamos viviendo
estáis hablando	estáis comiendo	estáis viviendo
están hablando	están comiendo	están viviendo

Ramón está bebiendo vino.
Ramón is drinking wine.
El gato está subiendo al árbol.
The cat is going up the tree.
Estoy aprendiendo francés.
I am learning French.

This tense has a more restricted use in Spanish than in English. It generally indicates an action taking place at the time of speaking.

IMITATED PRONUNCIATION (19)

ah-'blahn-do; ko-me-'en-do; vee-ve-'en-do; rrah-'mon; bay-be-'en-do; 'gah-to; soo-be-'en-do;ah-pren-de-'en-do; frahn-'thess.

20 INTERROGATIVE PRONOUNS: WHAT?, WHO? WHOSE?, ETC

3

¿Qué? What?
¿Quién? ¿Quiénes? (pl.) Who? Whom?
¿De quién? Whose?
¿Cuál? ¿Cuáles? (pl.) Which? What?

¿Qué come Vd.? What do you eat?
¿Quién es Vd.? Who are you?
¿De quién es esta pluma? Whose is this pen?

¿Cuál de estos trenes va a Valencia?
Which of these trains goes to Valencia?
¿Cuál es su nombre?
What is your name?

¿Qué? can sometimes play the role of an adjective:

¿Qué libros desea Vd.? Which books do you want?

IMITATED PRONUNCIATION (20)

kay; ke-'en; ke-'en-ess; day ke-'en; koo''ahl; koo''ahl-ess.

21 RELATIVE PRONOUNS: WHO, WHICH, THAT, ETC

1 que (who, which, that)

This can refer to persons or things, singular or plural, subject or object. Preceded by a preposition, **que** refers only to things. For example:

La chica que cuida a los niños.
The girl who looks after the children.
El coche que conduce.
The car he drives.
La casa en que vivimos.
The house in which we live.

2 quien, quienes (who, whom)

This refers only to persons, subject or object, and is used mainly after prepositions. It is also used after parts of the verb 'to be' and a noun or pronoun.

For example:
El profesor con quien estudio.
The teacher with whom I study.
El hombre para quien trabaja.
The man for whom he works.
Es él quien tiene la culpa.
It is he who is to blame.
Es María quien tiene que escribir.
It is Maria who has to write.

3 el que, la que, los que, las que, and **el cual, la cual, los cuales, las cuales** (who, whom, which, that)

These can refer to persons or things, subject or object, and are generally used after prepositions:

La mujer con la que está hablando.
The woman with whom he is speaking.
El autobús en el que viajo.
The bus in which I travel.
Los amigos de los cuales hablábamos.
The friends of whom we were talking.

el que, la que, los que, las que also translate 'he who', 'she who', 'those who', or 'the one/ones who':

El que acaba de llegar es su hijo.
The one who has just arrived is his son.
Los que han venido son todos estudiantes.
Those who have come are all students.

4 cuyo, cuya, cuyos, cuyas (whose, of whom, of which)

These are relative adjectives and agree with the noun they qualify:

El hombre cuya hija es actriz.
The man whose daughter is an actress.
La novela cuyo título no recuerdo.
The novel whose title I don't remember.

5 lo que/lo cual (what, which) refers to a clause or an idea

No comprendo lo que dice.
I don't understand what he says.
No ha llegado todavía, lo cual me sorprende.
He hasn't arrived yet, which surprises me.

Note that the relative pronoun can never be omitted in Spanish (as it often is in English):

El hombre a quien quiero ver.
The man I want to see.
El periódico que lee.
The newspaper he reads.

IMITATED PRONUNCIATION (21)

kay; koo''ee-dah; kon-'doo-**th**ay; ke-'en: ke-'en-ess;
pro-fay-'sorr; 'kool-pah; el kay, el koo''ahl etc;
ve''ah-Ho; ah-'kah-bah; ess-too-de-'ahn-tess;
'koo-yah etc; ac-'tree**th**; no-'vay-lah; 'tee-too-lo;
rray-koo''air-do; lo kay; lo koo''ahl; 'dee-**th**ay;
to-dah-'vee-ah; sorr-'pren-day; ke-'ay-ro vairr; 'lay-ay

VOCABULARY

el pueblo	village
la tienda	shop
leer (leyendo)	to read (reading)
el médico	doctor
la carta	letter
verde	green
la puerta	door
la pluma	pen
con	with
el número	number

3

IMITATED PRONUNCIATION

poo''ay-blo; te-'en-dah; lay-'airr; lay-'en-do; 'may-de-ko; 'kahrr-tah; 'vairr-day; poo''air-tah; 'ploo-mah; kon; 'noo-may-ro.

Exercise 13

Translate:

1 The village in which we live.
2 The woman who works in the shop.
3 The book that I have to read.
4 The town of which we are speaking.
5 It is Pedro who is (a) doctor.
6 Whose letters are these?
7 Which magazine is he buying?
8 The house which has a green door.
9 The pen with which I write.
10 What is the number?

Drills 2–4

Example:

¿Son Vds. norte americanos? Are you (pl.) American?
Sí, somos norte americanos. Yes, we're American.
¿Es Vd. norte americana? Are you American?
Sí, soy norte americana. Yes, I'm American.

1 ¿Beben Vds. cerveza?
2 ¿Come Vd. pan?
3 ¿Viven Vds. en Boston?
4 ¿Es Vd. médico?
5 ¿Hablan Vds. español?
6 ¿Compra Vd. la revista?

Example:

¿Es Vd. inglés? Are you English?
No, no soy inglés. No, I'm not English.
¿Son Vds. ingleses? Are you (pl.) English?
No, no somos ingleses. No, we're not English.

1 ¿Vive Vd. en Barcelona?
2 ¿Fuman Vds.?
3 ¿Aprende Vd. alemán?
4 ¿Compran Vds. los periódicos?
5 ¿Bebe Vd. vino?
6 ¿Son Vds. españoles?

Replace the blanks by the correct form of the present continuous. Example:
¿Qué come? Está comiendo pan.

1 ¿Qué compra? ... el periódico.
2 ¿Qué beben? ... cerveza.
3 ¿Qué estudia Vd.? ... español.
4 ¿Qué comen Vds.?... uvas.
5 ¿Qué lee? ... una revista.
6 ¿Qué hablan Vds.? ... inglés.
7 ¿Qué escribe? ... una carta.
8 ¿Qué aprenden? ... español.
9 ¿Qué sube Vd.? ... las maletas.

CONVERSATION

En la librería

DEPENDIENTA	**Buenos días, señor. ¿Qué desea?**
CLIENTE	**Buenos días. ¿Tiene Vd. un libro de historia de España?**
DEPENDIENTA	**Sí, señor, tenemos varios. Este es muy bueno, tiene muchas ilustraciones.**
CLIENTE	**Sí, parece muy interesante. ¿Cuánto es?**
DEPENDIENTA	**Doce euros.**
CLIENTE	**Es un poco caro. Y ése ¿cuánto es?**
DEPENDIENTA	**Ése, diez euros.**
CLIENTE	**Muy bien, ése por favor.**

TRANSLATION

At the bookshop

SHOP ASSISTANT	Good morning, Sir. Can I help you?
CUSTOMER	Good morning. Have you a book on the history of Spain?
SHOP ASSISTANT	Yes, Sir, we have several. This one is very good, it has many illustrations.
CUSTOMER	Yes, it looks very interesting. How much is it?
SHOP ASSISTANT	Twelve euros.
CUSTOMER	It is a little expensive. And that one, how much is it?
SHOP ASSISTANT	That one, ten euros.
CUSTOMER	All right, that one please.

3

Week 4

4

22 POSSESSIVE ADJECTIVES: MY, YOUR, ETC

	singular	plural
my	**mi**	**mis**
your	**tu**	**tus**
his, her, its, your (pol.)	**su**	**sus**
our	**nuestro (-a)**	**nuestros (-as)**
your	**vuestro (-a)**	**vuestros (-as)**
their, your (pol.)	**su**	**sus**

Possessive adjectives agree with the thing possessed, not with the possessor:

Mi coche	My car
Mis hermanos	My brothers
Nuestro perro	Our dog
Nuestras hijas	Our daughters

Although 'his', 'her', 'its', 'their', and 'your' are all translated by the forms **su** and **sus**, the meaning is usually clear from the context. However, in cases of ambiguity the following forms can be used: **de él, de ella, de ellos, de ellas, de Vd., de Vds.**

For example:

El libro de Vd	Your book
El amigo de ellos	Their friend

VOCABULARY

el hermano	brother
la hermana	sister
el tío	uncle
la tía	aunt
el marido	husband
la mujer	wife
el primo	cousin (m.)
la prima	cousin (f.)
el sobrino	nephew
la sobrina	niece
los padres	parents
los parientes	relatives

4

IMITATED PRONUNCIATION (22)

me; mees; too; toos; soo; sooss, etc; airr-'mahn-o;
airr-'mahn-ah; 'tee-o; 'tee-ah; mah-'ree-do; moo-'Hairr;
'pree-mo; 'pree-mah; so-'bree-no; so-'bree-nah;
'pah-drace; pah-re-'en-tace.

Exercise 14

Translate:

1 My husband.

2 Her brother.

3 Our sister.

4 Their nephew.

5 His uncle.

6 My parents.

7 Your wife.

8 Their sons.

9 Your (pol.s.) cousin (m.).

10 His relatives.

	singular	plural
mine	el mío, la mía	los míos, las mías
yours	el tuyo, la tuya	los tuyos, las tuyas
his, hers, its, yours (pol.)	el suyo, la suya	los suyos, las suyas
ours	el nuestro, la nuestra	los nuestros, las nuestras
yours	el vuestro, la vuestra	los vuestros, las vuestras
theirs, yours (pol.)	el suyo, la suya	los suyos, las suyas

Possessive pronouns agree in gender and number with the noun they replace. They are always preceded by the definite article, except after the verb **ser** when the article is usually omitted.

For example:
Mi casa y la tuya My house and yours
Estas cartas son nuestras. These letters are ours.

These forms are also used as adjectives, after the noun and without the article:

1 for emphasis:

¿Cuál es el coche vuestro?
Which is *your* car?

2 for direct address (as in letters):

Muy señor mío Dear Sir

3 to translate 'of mine', 'of yours', etc:

Un amigo mío A friend of mine
Una idea suya An idea of his

IMITATED PRONUNCIATION (23)

'me'o; me 'ah; 'me-os; 'me-ahs; 'too-yo, etc; 'soo-yo, etc.

Exercise 15

Replace the word in brackets with the appropriate form of the possessive pronoun:

1 Mi casa y (yours, fam.s.).
2 Nuestro jardín y (theirs).
3 Su coche y (ours).
4 Mi mujer y (his).
5 Vuestra madre y (ours).
6 Su padre y (mine).
7 Mi cerveza y (yours, pol.).
8 Nuestros amigos y (yours, fam.pl.).
9 Su secretaria y (mine).
10 Tu gato y (hers).

4

1	uno (m.), una (f.)	50	cincuenta
2	dos	60	sesenta
3	tres	70	setenta
4	cuatro	80	ochenta
5	cinco	90	noventa
6	seis	100	cien, ciento
7	siete	101	ciento uno (-a)
8	ocho	102	ciento dos
9	nueve	200	doscientos (-as)
10	diez	300	trescientos (-as)
11	once	400	cuatrocientos (-as)
12	doce	500	quinientos (-as)
13	trece	600	seiscientos (-as)
14	catorce	700	setecientos (-as)
15	quince	800	ochocientos (-as)
16	dieciséis	900	novecientos (-as)
17	diecisiete	1,000	mil
18	dieciocho	1,001	mil uno (-a)
19	diecinueve	1,002	mil dos
20	veinte	1,100	mil cien
21	veintiuno(-a)	1,101	mil ciento uno (-a)
22	veintidós	1,200	mil doscientos (-as)
23	veintitrés, etc.	2,000	dos mil
30	treinta	100,000	cien mil
31	treinta y uno (-a)	200,000	doscientos mil
32	treinta y dos	1,000,000	un millón
40	cuarenta	2,000,000	dos millones

IMITATED PRONUNCIATION (24)

'oo-no; 'oo-nah; doss; tress; koo''ah-tro; 'thin-ko;
'say-iss; se-'ay-tay; 'o-cho; noo''ay-vay; de- 'eth;
'on-thay; 'do-thay; 'tray-thay; kah-'torr-thay;
'kin-thay; de-'eth-e-'say-iss, etc; (20) 'vay'n-tay;
'vay'n-te-'oo-no, etc; (30) 'tray-in-tah, etc;
(40) koo'ah-'ren-tah; thin-koo''en-tah; say-'sen-tah;
say-'ten-tah; o-'chen-tah; no-'ven-tah; the-'en;
the-'en-to, etc; (1000) meel; (1,000,000) mee-'l'yon.

Uno and **ciento** are contracted to **un** and **cien** in front of a noun or an adjective:

un libro   one book
cien libros   a hundred books

Exercise 16

Translate:

1 Ten houses.

2 Seventy two euros.

3 Two hundred women.

4 Sixteen letters.

5 One hundred and thirty five books.

6 Forty six hotels.

7 Three hundred and fifty four apples.

8 Sixty eight shops.

9 One thousand four hundred men.

10 Seven hundred and eighty five cars.

25 ORDINAL NUMBERS: FIRST, SECOND, ETC

1st	primero	6th	sexto
2nd	segundo	7th	séptimo
3rd	tercero	8th	octavo
4th	cuarto	9th	noveno
5th	quinto	10th	décimo

Beyond the 'tenth', cardinal numbers are generally used:

Felipe II (segundo)	Philip II
Alfonso XII (doce)	Alfonso XII
El siglo III (tercero)	The third century
El siglo XX (veinte)	The twentieth century
El octavo piso	The eighth floor
El piso trece	The thirteenth floor

Note that with titles and centuries both ordinal and cardinal numbers follow the noun.

All the ordinal numbers form their feminine and plural in the usual way:

La tercera vez The third time
Los primeros días The first days

Primero and **tercero** are shortened to **primer** and **tercer** in front of the masculine noun:

El primer hombre The first man
El tercer niño The third child

IMITATED PRONUNCIATION (25)

pre-'may-ro; say-'goon-do; tairr-'**th**ay-ro; koo''ar-to; 'keen-to; 'sex-to; 'sep-te-mo; ock-'tah-vo; no-'vay-no; 'day-**th**e-mo; fay-'lee-pay; ahl-'fon-so; 'see-glo; 'pee-so; ve**th**; 'dee-ahss; pree-'mairr; tairr-'**th**airr.

Exercise 17

Translate:

1 The seventh book.
2 The first wife.
3 The third daughter.
4 The sixth son.
5 The second door.
6 The tenth day.
7 The fourth street.
8 The ninth child.
9 The fifth man.
10 The eighth shop.

26 THE TIME

Telling the time is quite easy, as the following examples show:

¿Qué hora es? What is the time?
Es la una. It is one o'clock.
Son las dos. It is two o'clock.
Son las tres. It is three o'clock.

Notice that the feminine article is used because it stands for the unsaid **hora**, and the plural form (in verb as well as article) applies in all hours except 'one'.

'Quarter to' is expressed by **menos cuarto**, 'quarter past' by **y cuarto**, and 'half past' by **y media**.

For example:
Son las siete y diez. It is ten past seven.
Es la una menos veinte. It is twenty to one.
Son las ocho y media. It is half past eight.
Son las cinco menos cuarto. It is quarter to five.
Son las nueve y cuarto. It is quarter past nine.

Mediodía is 'midday' and **medianoche** is 'midnight'. If you want to be exact, **a las once en punto** means 'at eleven o'clock precisely'. **A eso de** means 'at about ...'.

'a.m.' is expressed by **de la mañana** and 'p.m.' by **de la tarde** or **de la noche** (use the latter for the times after 8.30 p.m.).

For example:
El tren sale a las nueve de la mañana.
The train leaves at 9 a.m.
En España comemos a eso de las dos de la tarde.
In Spain we have lunch at about 2 p.m.
Pedro llega a su casa a las once de la noche.
Peter arrives at his house at 11 p.m.

The expressions **por la mañana** ('in the morning'), **por la tarde** ('in the afternoon', 'in the evening'), and **por la noche** ('at night') are used when the time of day is not given:

Ramón trabaja por la mañana.
Ramon works in the morning.
Leo en el jardín por la tarde.
I read in the garden in the afternoon.
Por la noche todo está en silencio.
At night everything is silent.

IMITATED PRONUNCIATION (26)

kay 'o-rah ess; 'may-nos koo''ar-to; ee 'may-de-ah;
may-de-o-'dee-ah; may-de-ah-'no-chay;
mah-n''yah-nah; 'tarr-day; 'no-chay.

27 DAYS OF THE WEEK, TIME EXPRESSIONS

The days of the week (which in Spanish do not begin with a capital letter) are:

lunes	Monday
martes	Tuesday
miércoles	Wednesday
jueves	Thursday
viernes	Friday
sábado	Saturday
domingo	Sunday

The days of the week are always preceded by the definite article **el**.

For example:
El domingo por la mañana
Sunday morning

Some useful expressions of time:

ayer	yesterday
anteayer	the day before yesterday
hoy	today
hoy día	nowadays
mañana	tomorrow
pasado mañana	the day after tomorrow
mañana por la mañana	tomorrow morning
mañana por la tarde	tomorrow afternoon/evening
mañana por la noche	tomorrow night
de día	by day
de noche	by night
al día siguiente	on the following day
un día sí y otro no	every other day
a los pocos días	a few days later
hace unos días	a few days ago

IMITATED PRONUNCIATION (27)

'loo-ness; 'mar-tess; me-'air-co-less; Hoo-'ay-vess;
ve-'air-ness; 'sah-bah-do; do-'min-go; ah-'yair;
ahn-tay-ah-'yair; 'o'e; 'o'e 'dee-ah; mah-n''yah-nah;
pah-'sah-do; 'no-chay; se-ghee-'en-tay.

28 MONTHS OF THE YEAR

The months of the year, which are also spelt with a small
initial letter in Spanish, are:

enero	January	**julio**	July
febrero	February	**agosto**	August
marzo	March	**septiembre**	September
abril	April	**octubre**	October
mayo	May	**noviembre**	November
junio	June	**diciembre**	December

29 SEASONS OF THE YEAR

The seasons of the year are:

la primavera	spring
el verano	summer
el otoño	autumn
el invierno	winter

The Spanish seasons are never spelt with an initial capital, as sometimes is the case in English.

IMITATED PRONUNCIATION (28/29)

ay-'nay-ro; fay-'bray-ro; 'mar-**th**o; ah-'bril; 'mah-yo; 'Hoo-ne-o; 'Hoo-le-o; ah-'gos-to; sep-te-'em-bray; ok-'too-bray; no-ve-'em-bray; dee-**th**e-'em-bray; pre-mah-'vay-rah; vay-'rah-no; o-'to-n'yo; in-ve-'air-no.

30 DATES

The date can be expressed in two different ways:

1 with the verb **estar**

¿A cuántos estamos?
What is the date?

2 with the verb **ser**

¿Qué fecha es hoy?
What is the date today?
Estamos a siete *or* **Es el siete.**
It's the seventh.

The ordinal number is used for the first of the month, the cardinal numbers for the rest:

El primero de mayo
The first of May

El quince de octubre
The fifteenth of October
[Nació] el cuatro de abril de mil novecientos dos.
[He was born on] the 4th April 1902.

VOCABULARY

hasta	until
frío	cold
las vacaciones	holidays
el cumpleaños	birthday
generalmente	usually
ir	to go
cenar	to have dinner
el reloj	watch, clock

IMITATED PRONUNCIATION (30)

'fay-chah; nah-**th**e-'o; 'ahs-tah; 'free-o;
vah-kah-**th**e-'o-ness; koom-play-'ah-n'yos;
Hay-nay-rahl-'men-tay; eer; **th**ay-'narr; rray-'loH.

Exercise 18

Translate:

1 What is the time?
2 It is twenty past ten on my watch.
3 I work until half past eleven.
4 The winter in Madrid is cold.
5 They have their holidays in July.
6 My birthday is (on) the 3rd of January.
7 He is free on Saturdays.
8 October is usually a beautiful month.
9 We have to go to Barcelona in May.
10 On Sundays I have dinner with my parents.

4

Juan y Carmen trabajan en la misma oficina

JUAN **Oye, Carmen, el sábado doy una pequeña fiesta en mi casa.**

CARMEN **¡Ah, qué bien!**

JUAN **Es mi cumpleaños y quiero celebrarlo.**

CARMEN **Así que tu cumpleaños es en junio. El mío también. ¡Qué casualidad!**

JUAN **¿En qué fecha es el tuyo?**

CARMEN **El dieciocho.**

JUAN **Tres días después del mío, entonces. Bueno, ¿puedes venir a mi fiesta?**

CARMEN **¿A qué hora es?**

JUAN **A las ocho.**

CARMEN **Me gustaría, pero el sábado tengo que trabajar horas extraordinarias hasta las nueve y media.**

JUAN **No te preocupes porque la fiesta dura hasta la una o las dos de la mañana.**

CARMEN **En ese caso acepto. ¿Has invitado a mucha gente?**

JUAN **No, doce o catorce amigos, porque mi casa no es muy grande. Hasta el sábado, entonces.**

CARMEN **Adiós y gracias por invitarme.**

Juan and Carmen work in the same office

JUAN   Listen, Carmen, on Saturday I am giving a little party at home.

CARMEN   How nice!

JUAN   It's my birthday and I want to celebrate.

CARMEN   So, your birthday is in June. Mine too. What a coincidence!

JUAN   What date is yours?

CARMEN   The eighteenth.

JUAN   Three days after mine, then. Well, can you come to my party?

CARMEN   At what time?

JUAN   At eight o'clock.

CARMEN   I'd like to, but on Saturday I have to work overtime until nine thirty.

JUAN   Don't worry because the party goes on until one or two in the morning.

CARMEN   In that case I accept. Have you invited many people?

JUAN   No, twelve or fourteen friends because my house is not very big. Until Saturday then.

CARMEN   Goodbye and thank you for inviting me.

4

Revision exercises 1

Exercise 1

Fill in the blanks, choosing a verb from the column on the right:

1	Sólo … un billete de diez euros.	habla
2	Carmen y Pedro … en Barcelona.	aprende
3	Mi hermana … secretaria.	son
4	¿Dónde … los periódicos?	cena
5	Los niños no … mucho pan.	viven
6	Es italiano pero … español.	trabajamos
7	Estos zapatos … muy caros.	es
8	Ramón … generalmente a las nueve.	están
9	Mi primo … francés y alemán.	comen
10	Nosotros no … los sábados.	tengo

Exercise 2

Translate:

1 In Spain, American newspapers are very expensive.
2 Where are the suitcases?
3 The room is on the third floor.
4 In the summer they live in England and in winter they live in Spain.
5 Her husband is ill, he drinks too much.
6 I have to write to my German friend (f.).
7 These flowers are for John's mother.
8 Mrs. Suarez is a charming woman.
9 We have to buy the tickets.
10 What is the time? Quarter past seven.
11 Is that dog yours (pol.)?
12 Our daughter is learning Spanish.

Exercise 3

Answer the following questions by translating the sentences shown in English:

1 ¿De dónde eres?
   I am American.

2 ¿Entonces vives en Washington?
   No, I live in Boston.

3 ¿Por qué estás en España?
   I am on holiday.

4 ¿Cuántas semanas de vacaciones tienes?
   Only two.

5 ¿Trabajas?
   Yes, I work in a shop.

6 ¿Qué clase de tienda?
   It's a bookshop.

7 ¿Estás en un hotel?
   No, I am at a friend's (f.) house.

8 ¿Dónde vive tu amiga?
   In a house on the beach.

9 ¿Tienes sed? ¿Quieres (would you like) una cerveza?
   No, thank you, I am in a hurry. Goodbye.

4

Week 5

- *the verb 'ir', 'to go'*
- *the past participle and the perfect tense (introducing 'haber', 'to have')*
- *how to translate 'there is' and 'there are'*
- *personal pronouns used as direct and indirect objects ('me', 'to me', 'you', 'to you', etc)*
- *the imperative*

31 THE VERB 'IR' ('TO GO')

This is an irregular verb. Its present tense is as follows:

voy	**vamos**
vas	**vais**
va	**van**

Ir a translates 'to go to' and 'to be going to', e.g.:

Van a la iglesia.
They go to church.
Voy a comprar un periódico.
I am going to buy a newspaper.

The 1st person plural **vamos** translates 'let's' as well as 'we go to' and 'we are going to'. The meaning is usually clear from the context:

Vamos al cine todos los viernes.
We go to the cinema every Friday.
Vamos a comprar los billetes.
We are going to buy the tickets.
Vamos a ver.
Let's see.

Exercise 19

Translate:

1 We go to church on Sundays.
2 I am going to buy that book.
3 He goes to his friend's house.
4 We go on holiday in the summer.
5 They go to Madrid by train.
6 Let's have a coffee.
7 She is not going to sing.
8 Tomorrow I am going to have a rest.
9 They go shopping in the market.
10 Let's go to the theatre.

32 THE PAST PARTICIPLE ('SPOKEN', 'EATEN')

The past participle of regular verbs is formed by adding
-**ado** to verbs ending in -**ar**, and -**ido** to verbs ending in
-**er** and -**ir**.

hablar→ **hablado** (spoken)
comer→ **comido** (eaten)
vivir→ **vivido** (lived)

There are some irregular past participles. Here are a few
examples:

escribir (to write)→ **escrito** (written)
ver (to see)→ **visto** (seen)
hacer (to do, to make)→ **hecho** (done, made)
decir (to say, to tell)→ **dicho** (said, told)

33 THE PERFECT TENSE ('I HAVE DONE')

This tense is formed with the present indicative of **haber**
(to have) followed by the past participle of the appropriate
verb. For example, the perfect tense of the verb
comprar (to buy) is:

he comprado	I have bought
has comprado	you have bought
ha comprado	he has bought
hemos comprado	we have bought
habéis comprado	you have bought
han comprado	they have bought

Haber is an auxiliary verb and is never used as a
synonym of **tener**.

The use of the perfect tense in Spanish is similar to that
in English:

Hemos viajado todo el día.
We have travelled all day.

Note that the auxiliary and the past participle must not be separated in Spanish:

Siempre he trabajado.
I have always worked.

34 'HAY' ('THERE IS', 'THERE ARE')

'There is' and 'there are' are rendered by **hay**, which is an impersonal form of the verb **haber**. Note that **hay** has no plural:

Hay una barca en la playa.
There is a boat on the beach.
Hay muchos turistas en esta ciudad.
There are many tourists in this town.

Hay que followed by an infinitive is usually translated by 'one must' or 'you must':

Hay que ver la catedral.
You must see the cathedral.
No hay que llorar.
One mustn't cry.

'There has been' and 'there have been' are rendered by the 3rd person singular of the perfect tense of the verb **haber (ha habido)**:

Ha habido un accidente de carretera.
There has been a road accident.
Ha habido muchos problemas.
There have been many problems.

5

5

Exercise 20

Translate:

1 I have written three letters.
2 They have spoken in Spanish.
3 We have eaten too much.
4 There is sugar in this tea.
5 She has bought a new dress.
6 Have you finished the job?
7 He has never helped in the house.
8 There are some oranges in the bag.
9 Have you (pol. sing.) drunk the beer?
10 I haven't seen the movie.

All verbs except **tener** are followed by the preposition **a** when the direct object is a definite person or animal:

Llamo a Pedro. I call Peter.
Llamo a mi perro. I call my dog.
but
Tiene un perro. He has a dog.
Compra el libro. He buys the book.

VOCABULARY

visitar	to visit
llamar	to call
preparar	to prepare
la comida	meal, food
invitar	to invite
casado (-a)	married
el caballo	horse
bañar	to bathe
esperar	to wait for, to expect
el profesor	teacher

5

Exercise 21

Rewrite the following sentences filling in the blanks with the personal 'a' where necessary:

1 Voy a ver … mi tío.
2 Tenemos que ayudar … nuestros amigos.
3 Juan ha comprado … un perro.
4 No he hablado … el médico.
5 Está leyendo … el periódico.
6 Vamos a invitar … Pedro.
7 Tengo … tres hermanos.
8 Esperamos … una carta de María.
9 Voy a beber … una cerveza.
10 Están llamando … su hija.

Exercise 22

Translate:

1 He visits his mother.
2 I have seen the woman.
3 We have to call the dogs.
4 María prepares the meal.
5 They have invited their friends.
6 She has a married sister.
7 I am going to buy a horse.
8 We have to bathe the child.
9 They are waiting for the teacher.
10 Carlos has not seen Toledo.

5

36 DIRECT AND INDIRECT OBJECT PRONOUNS: ME, HIM, TO ME, TO HIM, ETC

Direct object

me	me
te	you (fam.)
le	him, you (pol.m.)
la	her, you (pol.f.)
lo, la	it (m.), it (f.)
nos	us
os	you (fam.)
les	them, you (pol.m.)
las	them, you (pol.f.)
los, las	them (m., f.) referring to things.

Indirect object

me	to me
te	to you
le	to him, to her, to it, to you (pol.)
nos	to us
os	to you
les	to them, to you (pol.)

Object pronouns usually precede the verb:

Nos ayuda con el trabajo. He helps us with the work.
Le he escrito una carta. I have written him a letter.

When the verb is an infinitive, a present participle or an imperative, the pronoun is usually added to the end of the verb:

Tengo que comprarlo. I have to buy it.
Está esperándome. He is waiting for me.
Bébalo. Drink it.

If the infinitive or present participle is preceded by another verb, as it is in the case of the above examples, the object pronoun may be placed before that verb:

Lo tengo que comprar. I have to buy it.
Me está esperando. He is waiting for me.

When an object pronoun is added to the present participle, an accent must be used so that the stress still falls on the same syllable:

Está bebiéndolo. He is drinking it.
Estamos terminándolo. We are finishing it.

37 ORDER OF PRONOUNS ('HE GIVES IT TO ME')

When two object pronouns come together, the indirect object pronoun is always placed first:

Me lo da. He gives it to me.
Nos la lee. He reads it to us.

When two pronouns of the third person come together, the indirect object pronoun **le/les** becomes **se**:

Se la envía. He sends it to him.

In order to avoid any possible ambiguity in the meaning of **le**, **les**, or **se**, you may add **a él, a ellas, a Vd.**, etc after the verb:

Le escribo la carta a él. I write the letter to him.
Les compro flores a ellas. I buy them flowers.
Se lo he dado a Vd. I have given it to you.

37A REDUNDANT USE OF OBJECT PRONOUNS

Sometimes for emphasis the noun or pronoun which is the object or indirect object of the sentence precedes the verb. When this happens, the corresponding object pronoun must also be used immediately before the verb.

For example:
A esos amigos les veo poco.
I don't see much of those friends.
A Juan le he comprado una corbata.
For Juan, I have bought a tie.
A nosotros no nos han invitado.
They haven't invited us.

Even when the indirect object noun or pronoun follows the verb, the corresponding object pronoun is often inserted before the verb. This is especially common in conversational Spanish:

Se lo he dicho a Pedro. I have told Pedro.

VOCABULARY

ofrecer	to offer
la taza	cup
enviar	to send
la carne	meat
el pescado	fish
comprender	to understand
vender	to sell
la bicicleta	bicycle

5

Exercise 23

Replace the words in brackets by the appropriate form of the object pronoun:

1 Juan ofrece (el pan) (a su amigo).

2 Bebo (una taza de té) por la mañana.

3 Hemos comprado (un coche).

4 Me ha enviado (unas flores).

5 He escrito (una carta) (a mi tía).

6 Comemos (la carne y el pescado).

7 Estos señores no comprenden (el inglés).

8 Tengo que estudiar (la lección).

9 Nos ha vendido (las bicicletas).

10 Hemos dado (los libros) (a Pedro).

38 THE IMPERATIVE: POLITE COMMANDS

In regular verbs, the polite imperative is formed by adding the following endings to the stem:

	singular	plural
	-e	-en to verbs ending in -ar
	-a	-an to verbs ending in -er and -ir

hablar	hable Vd.	hablen Vds. (speak)
comer	coma Vd.	coman Vds. (eat)
subir	suba Vd.	suban Vds. (go up)

Vd. is usually added to the polite form of the imperative.

Object pronouns are placed after the imperative unless it is negative:

Bébalo Vd. Drink it.
No lo beba Vd. Don't drink it.
Envíeselo Vd. Send it to him.
No se lo envíe Vd. Don't send it to him.

In irregular verbs the polite imperative is usually formed by adding the same endings as for regular verbs (shown above) to the stem of the first person singular of the present tense:

	present	imperative
tener (to have)	**tengo**	**tenga Vd./tengan Vds.**
decir (to say)	**digo**	**diga Vd./digan Vds.**
contar (to count)	**cuento**	**cuente Vd./cuenten Vds.**

Note the irregular forms of **ir**: **vaya Vd./vayan Vds.**

Exercise 24

Translate:

1 Don't smoke.
2 Drink this wine.
3 Send me the magazine.
4 Read them the letter.
5 Sell him your watch.
6 Learn these numbers.
7 Write your name here.
8 Don't eat those apples.
9 Don't buy that meat.
10 Don't give them to me.

Repeat the exercise, putting the imperative in the plural.

Drills 5–6

Example:
¿Ha tomado Vd. el café? Have you had the coffee?
No, voy a tomarlo ahora. No, I'm going to have it now.

1 ¿Ha tomado Vd. la cerveza?
2 ¿Han ido de compras?
3 ¿Ha escrito la carta?
4 ¿Han hecho Vds. el trabajo?
5 ¿Ha comprado Vd. los libros?
6 ¿Han visto a su padre?
7 ¿Han terminado Vds. la comida?
8 ¿Ha llamado a Conchita?
9 ¿Ha subido Vd. las maletas?
10 ¿Han bebido Vds. el vino?

Example:
¿Preparo la comida? Shall I prepare the meal?
Sí, prepárela. Yes, prepare it.

¿Preparamos la comida? Shall we prepare the meal?
Sí, prepárenla. Yes, prepare it.

1 ¿Compro el periódico?
2 ¿Subimos las maletas?
3 ¿Llamo al profesor?
4 ¿Invitamos a esos amigos?
5 ¿Leo la carta?
6 ¿Enviamos estas flores?
7 ¿Bebo esta cerveza?
8 ¿Vendemos esta bicicleta?

Drill 7

Example:
Beba Vd. el café. Drink the coffee.
Ya lo he bebido. I have already drunk it.
Beban Vds. el café. Drink the coffee.
Ya lo hemos bebido. We have already drunk it.

1 Prepare Vd. el pescado.
2 Llamen Vds. al perro.
3 Escriba Vd. su nombre.
4 Tomen Vds. la carne.
5 Compre Vd. los billetes.
6 Hablen Vds. a los profesores.
7 Cuente Vd. los libros.
8 Vendan Vds. el reloj.
9 Lea Vd. esta revista.

5

Un día muy ocupado

CARMEN   ¿Qué vas a hacer hoy?

ANTONIO   Hoy tengo varias cosas que hacer. Primero tengo que ir al banco, y después voy a ir a ver a Carlos que está en el hospital.

CARMEN   ¿En el hospital? ¿Qué le pasa?

ANTONIO   Ha tenido un accidente de automóvil volviendo de Málaga.

CARMEN   Y ¿ha sido muy grave?

ANTONIO   No. Tiene una pierna rota y dos o tres heridas leves.

CARMEN   ¡Pobre hombre! Tengo que llamar a su mujer y ofrecerle mi ayuda, si la necesita.

ANTONIO   Sí, esa es una buena idea.

CARMEN   Bueno, y por la tarde ¿qué vas a hacer?

ANTONIO   Tengo que pasarme por la oficina, pero no voy a estar mucho tiempo.

CARMEN   Entonces, ¿podemos ir al cine? Ponen una película francesa en el Roxy que deseo ver. Mi hermana la ha visto y me ha dicho que es muy buena.

ANTONIO   Pues, te espero a las siete menos cuarto en la puerta del cine. ¿Vale?

CARMEN   Muy bien.

5

A very busy day

CARMEN   What are you going to do today?

ANTONIO   Today I have several things to do. First I have to go to the bank, and then I am going to see Charles who is in hospital.

CARMEN   In hospital? What is the matter with him?

ANTONIO   He has had a car accident coming back from Málaga.

CARMEN   And was it very serious?

ANTONIO   No. He has a broken leg and two or three minor injuries.

CARMEN   Poor man! I must ring his wife and offer my help if she needs it.

ANTONIO   Yes, that's a good idea.

CARMEN   Right, and in the afternoon what are you going to do?

ANTONIO   I have to call in at the office, but I'm not going to be long.

CARMEN   In that case can we go to the cinema? They are showing a French film at the Roxy that I want to see. My sister has seen it and she has told me that it is very good.

ANTONIO   So ... I'll wait for you at a quarter to seven outside the cinema. All right?

CARMEN   Fine.

Week 6

- question words and exclamations
- verbs which change their spelling in the stem
- reflexive verbs ('to wash oneself')
- pronouns with prepositions
- some irregular present tenses
- idioms using 'hacer' ('to do', 'to make')
- impersonal verbs
- the verbs 'gustar' ('to like') and 'querer' ('to love', 'to want')

39 SOME USEFUL QUESTION WORDS

¿Dónde? ¿Adónde?	Where? Where (to)?
¿Cómo?	How?
¿Cuándo?	When?
¿Cuánto, -a, -os, -as?	How much? How many?
¿Por qué?	Why?

Note that **porque** written as one word means 'because'.
¿Verdad? (literally 'true') is used to seek corroboration
of a statement:

¿Dónde está la pluma?
Where is the pen?
¿Adónde van Vds.?
Where are you going?
¿Cómo está Vd.?
How are you?
¿Cuándo salimos?
When are we going out?
¿Cuántos libros necesitas?
How many books do you need?
¿Por qué no compras el coche?
Why don't you buy the car?
Porque no tengo dinero.
Because I have no money.
Conchita es muy simpática, ¿verdad?
Conchita is very nice, isn't she?

6

39A EXCLAMATIONS

¡Cómo!	What! How …!
¡Cuánto, -a, -os, -as!	How much …! What a lot …!
¡Qué!	What a …! How …!
¡Quién!	Would that I…/If only I …! (imperfect subjunctive)

¡Cómo pesa esta maleta!
How heavy this suitcase is!
¡Cómo! ¿No vas a venir a la fiesta?
What! You're not coming to the party?
¡Cuánto tenemos que hablar!
How much/What a lot we have to talk about!
¡Qué caras son estas manzanas!
How expensive these apples are!
¡Qué bonita iglesia!
What a lovely church!
¡Qué pena!
What a pity!
¡Qué amable!
How kind!
¡Qué asco!
How revolting!
¡Quién tuviera dinero!
If only I had money!

Note that if the noun that follows **¡Qué…!** is itself followed by an adjective, you need to insert either **tan** or **más** in front of the adjective:

¡Qué casa tan grande!
What a big house!
¡Qué mujer más trabajadora!
What a hard-working woman!
¡Qué niños tan traviesos!
How naughty the children are!

40 VERBS THAT CHANGE THEIR STEM

There are several Spanish verbs that change their stem vowels when the stress falls on them: e changes to ie, o changes to ue, and in some verbs of the third conjugation e changes to i.

present tenses

pensar	**volver**	**pedir**
to think	to return	to ask for

pienso	**vuelvo**	**pido**
piensas	**vuelves**	**pides**
piensa	**vuelve**	**pide**
pensamos	**volvemos**	**pedimos**
pensáis	**volvéis**	**pedís**
piensan	**vuelven**	**piden**

The first and second persons plural remain regular as the stem vowel is not stressed. Verbs that change their stem will be shown in subsequent vocabularies thus:

pensar (ie); volver (ue); pedir (i).

41 REFLEXIVE VERBS ('I WASH MYSELF')

When the object of the verb is the same person or thing as its subject the verb is called reflexive. These are much more common in Spanish than in English.

reflexive pronouns

me	myself
te	yourself
se	himself, herself, itself, yourself (pol.)
nos	ourselves
os	yourselves
se	themselves, yourselves (pol.pl.)

The third person of the reflexive pronoun, se, is attached to the infinitive of verbs which are reflexive:

lavarse	to wash oneself
sentarse (ie)	to sit down
dormirse (ue)	to go to sleep

Present tense of **lavarse**:
me lavo
te lavas
se lava
nos lavamos
os laváis
se lavan

Regarding their position, reflexive pronouns follow the same rules as object pronouns:

Me lavo. I wash myself.
Tengo que lavarme. I have to wash myself.
Estoy lavándome. I am washing myself.
Lávese Vd. Wash yourself.
No se lave Vd. Don't wash yourself.

Some verbs change their meaning when used reflexively:

llamar	to call
llamarse	to call oneself, to be called
ir	to go
irse	to go away
dormir	to sleep
dormirse	to go to sleep
llevar	to carry, to wear
llevarse	to take away

With some verbs the reflexive pronoun may be used to give emphasis or finality to the action of the verb:

decidir, decidirse a	to decide
morir, morirse (ue)	to die
parar, pararse	to stop

42 RECIPROCAL FORM ('WE LOVE EACH OTHER')

The reflexive pronoun is also used in reciprocal verbs such as:

quererse (ie)   to love each other
comprenderse   to understand each other
verse   to see each other

Mi hermano y yo no nos comprendemos.
My brother and I don't understand each other.

VOCABULARY

todos los días	every day
casarse	to get married
odiar(se)	to hate (each other)
ayudar(se)	to help (each other)
acostarse (ue)	to go to bed

6

Exercise 26

Translate:

1 Pedro and Anita write to each other every day.
2 The car is going to stop.
3 We are going to get married.
4 The children go to bed at eight o'clock.
5 We have to wash ourselves.
6 The two men hate each other.
7 He always asks me for money.
8 They never help each other.
9 Carlos returns from the office at half past six.
10 I must go to sleep.
11 Take away these cups!
12 The street is called Baeza.
13 I am going to sit here.
14 We are going away tomorrow.
15 I have decided to live in Spain.

6

The pronouns used after prepositions, known as disjunctive pronouns, are the same as subject pronouns, except for **mí** (me); **ti** (you, familiar); **sí** (himself, herself, yourself):

Estas cartas son para mí.
These letters are for me.
No vuelve con nosotros.
He does not come back with us.
Vamos sin ella.
We go without her.

With the preposition **con** ('with'), the forms **mí**, **ti**, and **sí** become **conmigo**, **contigo**, and **consigo**:

No puedo vivir contigo.
I cannot live with you.
Siempre lleva un libro consigo.
He always carries a book with him(self).

Consigo can only be used reflexively; otherwise the forms 'with him', 'with her', 'with you', 'with them', are translated by **con él, con ella, con Vd.**, etc.

VOCABULARY

el regalo	present
para	for
el tiempo	weather
contra	against
sin	without
siempre	always
el viaje	journey
entre	between
según	according to

Exercise 26

Translate:

1 We are working with them.
2 He has bought a present for me.
3 Is he going to come back with you (pol.s.)?
4 The weather is against us.
5 They have gone away without him.
6 He has always lived with me.
7 These letters are for her.
8 They are going to buy the house between them.
9 Are the children with you (fam.s.)?
10 According to him, the journey is too long.

44 IRREGULAR VERBS IN THE PRESENT TENSE

6

In their present tenses the following verbs are irregular only in the first person singular:

poner (to put)	**pongo, pones, pone, ponemos, ponéis, ponen**
salir (to go out)	**salgo, sales, sale, salimos, salís, salen**
ver (to see)	**veo, ves, ve, vemos, veis, ven**
hacer (to do, to make)	**hago, haces, hace, hacemos, hacéis, hacen**
traer (to bring)	**traigo, traes, trae, traemos, traéis, traen**
dar (to give)	**doy, das, da, damos, dais, dan**
saber (to know)	**sé, sabes, sabe, sabemos, sabéis, sabéis, saben**

45 IDIOMATIC USES OF 'HACER'

Besides translating 'to do', 'to make', **hacer** is used:

1 in a number of impersonal expressions relating to the weather

¿Qué tiempo hace? What's the weather like?
Hace frío. It's cold.
Hace (mucho) calor. It's (very) hot.
Hace sol. It's sunny.
Hace viento. It's windy.
Hace buen día. It's a nice day.

2 in certain expressions of time

Hace muchos años. Many years ago.
Hace media hora. Half an hour ago.
¿Hace mucho tiempo que esperas?
Have you been waiting long?

3 in some other idiomatic expressions

hacer(se) daño	to hurt oneself
no hacer caso	to ignore, not to take any notice
hacerse rico	to become rich
hacer señas	to motion
hacerse a algo	to become used to something

46 IMPERSONAL VERBS

llover (ue)	to rain
nevar (ie)	to snow
helar (ie)	to freeze
tronar (ue)	to thunder
amanecer	to dawn
anochecer	to get dark

47 THE VERB 'GUSTAR' ('TO LIKE')

This verb translates 'to like', 'to be keen on', but in the Spanish construction the English subject of the verb becomes the indirect object and the English object becomes the subject.

Me gusta el café. I like coffee.
Nos gusta Inglaterra. We like England.
Les gustan las uvas. They like grapes.
A Carlos le gusta pintar. Carlos likes painting.

When the subject of **gustar** is a verb, as in the sentence **A Carlos le gusta pintar**, the infinitive must always be used. Note also that the preposition **a** must be used in front of the noun which is the indirect object.

Sometimes a disjunctive pronoun is used for emphasis or to indicate a contrast. For example:

¿A Vd. le gusta el flamenco?
Do you like flamenco?
A mí no me gustan los deportes, pero a mi marido le gustan mucho.
I don't like sports, but my husband likes them very much.

There are other verbs which have the same construction in Spanish as **gustar**:

bastar (to suffice, to be enough)
Este dinero me basta. This money is enough for me.

faltar (to be missing, to be short of)
Siempre les falta tiempo. They are always short of time.

hacer falta (to need, to be necessary)
Nos hace falta más vino. We need more wine.

parecer (to seem, to think (of))
¿Qué te parecen estos pantalones?
What do you think of these trousers?

6

quedar (to remain, to have left)
¿Le quedan entradas para la función de la tarde?
Have you any tickets left for the evening performance?

sobrar (to be/to have more than enough)
Nos sobra tiempo para llegar a la estación.
We have more than enough time to get to the station.

Exercise 27

Translate:

1 What is the weather like?
2 Today it's very cold.
3 It's going to rain tomorrow.
4 I don't like this beer.
5 He is going to bring us coffee.
6 He likes to go out every evening.
7 I don't know where it is.
8 They go to Spain because they like the sun.
9 Twenty five years ago.
10 Carmen likes to sit in the garden.

48 THE VERB 'QUERER' (IE)

This verb means 'to love' (a person or animal) or 'to want', 'to wish'. It must not be confused with **gustar**, although the form **quisiera** (imperfect subjunctive) often translates the English 'I should like'.

Quiero a mis hijos. I love my children.
No quieren ir a Francia. They don't want to go to France.
Quisiera ver a Ramón. I should like to see Ramón.

Drills 8–9

Example:
¿Les gusta a Vds. España? Do you like Spain?
Sí, nos gusta mucho. Yes, we like it very much.

1 ¿Le gusta a Vd. la playa?
2 ¿Le gustan a Carlos los deportes?
3 ¿Les gusta a Vds. vivir en Madrid?
4 ¿Os gusta la cerveza?
5 ¿Le gusta a Conchita el regalo?
6 ¿Te gustan los niños?
7 ¿Le gusta a Vd. viajar?
8 ¿Les gusta a tus amigos el vino?
9 ¿Les gusta a Vds. el hotel?
10 ¿Les gusta a ellos el pescado?

Example:
Van Vds. con Carlos ¿verdad? You are going with
  Carlos, aren't you?
Sí, vamos con él. Yes, we are going with him.

1 Trabaja Vd. con María ¿verdad?
2 Esta carta es para nosotros ¿verdad?
3 Su hermano vuelve con Vd. ¿verdad?
4 Vamos al teatro sin los niños ¿verdad?
5 Estas flores son para mí ¿verdad?
6 Vive con sus padres ¿verdad?
7 Estos periódicos son para Vds. ¿verdad?
8 Va Vd. de compras sin su marido ¿verdad?

6

Drill 10

Example:

¿Quiere Vd. acostarse? Do you want to go to bed?
Sí, quisiera acostarme. Yes, I should like to go to bed.

¿Quieren Vds. acostarse? Do you want to go to bed?
Sí, quisiéramos acostarnos. Yes, we should like to go to bed.

1 ¿Quiere Vd. sentarse?   6 ¿Quieren Vds. sentarse?
2 ¿Quiere Vd. lavarse?   7 ¿Quieren Vds. lavarse?
3 ¿Quiere Vd. dormirse?   8 ¿Quieren Vds. dormirse?
4 ¿Quiere Vd. irse?   9 ¿Quieren Vds. irse?
5 ¿Quiere Vd. pararse?   10 ¿Quieren Vds. pararse?

6

CONVERSATION

Planes de vacaciones

MIGUEL **¿Adónde van Vds. de vacaciones este año?**

PILAR **Vamos a un pueblo de la costa del Mediterráneo, cerca de Valencia.**

MIGUEL **¿En qué mes van Vds.?**

PILAR **Vamos en julio porque hace muy buen tiempo. Hace calor y el mar está delicioso para bañarse.**

MIGUEL **A nosotros nos gusta más el norte. Todos los años vamos a Santander en agosto.**

PILAR **Pero en el norte hace mal tiempo, llueve mucho y hay muchos días en los que es imposible ir a la playa.**

MIGUEL **Es verdad. Pero no vamos buscando el sol, vamos huyendo del calor de Madrid que en agosto es insoportable.**

PILAR **Pues, a mí me gusta el calor. Ya tenemos bastante frío todo el invierno.**

MIGUEL **Yo, sin embargo, prefiero el invierno al verano.**

PILAR **Sobre gustos no hay nada escrito.**

Holiday plans

MIGUEL   Where are you going on holiday this year?

PILAR   We are going to a village on the Mediterranean coast, near Valencia.

MIGUEL   Which month do you go?

PILAR   We go in July because the weather is very good. It's warm and the sea is lovely to bathe in.

MIGUEL   We like the north better. Every year we go to Santander in August.

PILAR   But in the north the weather is bad, it rains a lot and there are many days when it's impossible to go to the beach.

MIGUEL   It's true. But we are not seeking the sun, we are running away from the heat in Madrid which, in August, is unbearable.

PILAR   Well, I like the hot weather. We are cold enough all through the winter.

MIGUEL   I, on the other hand, prefer winter to summer.

PILAR   There is no accounting for tastes.

6

Week 7

- *the imperfect tense ('was doing', 'used to do')*
- *the verb 'soler'*
- *the pluperfect tense ('had done')*
- *more negative words ('never', 'nothing', 'neither', etc)*
- *adverbs ('easily', 'frequently')*
- *comparison of adjectives, adverbs and nouns ('more ... than', 'less ... than', 'as ... as')*

49 THE IMPERFECT TENSE ('WAS DOING', 'USED TO DO')

The imperfect is used to express an habitual action, an action repeated over an indefinite period of time, with no beginning and no end. It translates the English 'was doing', 'used to do', but also sometimes 'did' and 'would' in the sense of 'used to'.

imperfect tenses

hablar	comer	vivir
hablaba	comía	vivía
hablabas	comías	vivías
hablaba	comía	vivía
hablábamos	comíamos	vivíamos
hablabais	comíais	vivíais
hablaban	comían	vivían

Carlos compraba el periódico todos los días.
Carlos used to buy the newspaper every day.
El hombre vendía caramelos.
The man was selling sweets.

As the first and third persons singular have the same forms, the subject pronoun is sometimes used to avoid ambiguity.

There are only three verbs which are irregular in the imperfect tense:

ser	ir	ver
to be	to go	to see

era	iba	veía
eras	ibas	veías
era	iba	veía
éramos	íbamos	veíamos
erais	ibais	veíais
eran	iban	veían

Íbamos a España una vez al año.
We used to go to Spain once a year.

'There was' and 'there were' are translated by **había** (the imperfect of the verb **haber**):

Había mucha gente en la playa.
There were a lot of people on the beach.
Había un embotellamiento en la plaza.
There was a traffic jam in the square.

50 THE VERB 'SOLER' (UE)

This is a verb only used in the present and imperfect. It is used to mean 'to be in the habit of', and for expressions where English has 'generally', 'usually', 'as a rule':

Suelo levantarme a las siete.
I usually get up at seven.
Solíamos ir de paseo los domingos.
We used to go for a walk on Sundays.

51 THE PLUPERFECT TENSE ('HAD DONE')

This is a compound tense and is formed with the imperfect of the auxiliary **haber** and the past participle of the appropriate verb. Thus:

Habíamos comido. We had eaten.
Habían escrito. They had written.
Ramón había salido. Ramón had gone out.

VOCABULARY

el gerente	manager
los bombones	chocolates
el muchacho	boy
buscar	to look for
la representación	performance
empezar (ie)	to begin
la fábrica	factory
el mar	sea
mirar	to look at

Exercise 28

Translate:

1 Luis was selling a car.
2 I usually see her in the morning.
3 They had spoken to the hotel manager.
4 He used to bring me chocolates.
5 The boy was looking for his suitcase.
6 The performance used to start at ten o'clock.
7 He had worked in a factory.
8 The sea was very cold.
9 The woman was looking at us.
10 We usually ate a lot of fish.

52 SOME NEGATIVE WORDS: NEVER, NOTHING, NEITHER, ETC

jamás, nunca	never
nada	nothing
tampoco	neither
nadie	no one, nobody
ninguno (-a)	none
ni ... ni	neither ... nor

Nunca sale de casa.
He never goes out of the house.
Nadie lo había visto.
Nobody had seen it.
Ni fuma, ni bebe.
He neither smokes, nor drinks.

However, the double negative is much more common in Spanish:

No necesito nada.
I don't need anything.
Mi padre no lo sabe tampoco.
My father doesn't know either.
No escribe nunca.
He never writes.

Ninguno (-a) can play the role of adjective or pronoun It may refer to people or things and it is always used in the singular. As an adjective the masculine form shortens to **ningún** in front of the noun:

No hay ningún niño en la playa.
There aren't any children on the beach.
Voy a comprar cigarrillos, no tengo ninguno.
I am going to buy cigarettes, I haven't any.

Corresponding to these negatives, there are the affirmative forms:

siempre	always
algo	something
también	also, too
alguien	someone, somebody
alguno (-a)	some, any
o … o	either … or

Alguien ha preguntado por Vd.
Somebody has asked for you.
O canta, o baila.
Either he sings, or he dances.

Alguno, like its opposite **ninguno**, shortens to **algún** in front of the masculine noun. It may sometimes be used in the singular when a plural form would be usual in English.

Quiero comprar algún periódico.
I want to buy some newspapers.

VOCABULARY

conocer	to know
la leche	milk
venir (ie)	to come
poder	to be able
ocurrir	to happen

7

Exercise 29

Fill in the blanks with the appropriate negative word:

1 Juan no quiere hacer ....
2 No conocemos a ... en esta ciudad.
3 No tienen ... pan ... leche.
4 María no viene ... a verme.
5 No he leído ... libro de Cervantes.
6 Carlos no puede ir y su hermano ....
7 ... sabe lo que ha ocurrido.
8 No hay ... nuevo.
9 No hemos comprado ... revista.
10 Esa mujer no ha trabajado ....

53 ADVERBS ('EASILY', 'FREQUENTLY')

Many adverbs are formed in Spanish by adding the ending **-mente** to the feminine form of the adjective:

maravillosamente wonderfully
fácilmente easily
frecuentemente frequently

When two or more adverbs ending in **-mente** follow one another, only the last one ends in **-mente**; the others keep the feminine form of the adjective:

El niño ha sido castigado justa y severamente.
The boy has been punished justly and severely.

In using some adverbs, there is an occasional pitfall or special construction to watch out for. Here are some examples.

1 ahora now

¿Qué vas a hacer ahora?
What are you going to do now?

2 ya now, already, (no) longer, yet (in a question)

Ya lo veo.
I can see now.
Ya han terminado de comer.
They have already finished eating.
Ya no vivimos en esa casa.
We no longer live in that house.
¿Se ha despertado ya?
Has he woken up yet?

Ya is often used simply for emphasis, and it is not translated in English:

¡Ya lo verás! You'll see!
¡Ya voy! I'm coming!
¡Ya lo creo! I should think so!

3 entonces then (at that time, in that case)

Yo trabajaba entonces en una compañía de seguros.
I was then working for an insurance company.
¿No quieres venir al cine? Entonces iré yo solo.
Don't you want to come to the cinema? Then I'll go alone/by myself.

4 luego then (next, soon after, later)

Primero tenemos que ir al banco y luego a la agencia de viajes.
First we have to go to the bank and then to the travel agent's.
¡Hasta luego!
See you later!
Desde luego.
Of course. Indeed!

Exercise 30

Form adverbs from the following adjectives:
1 feliz (happy).
2 verdadero (true).
3 triste (sad).
4 lento (slow).
5 nuevo (new).
6 agradable (pleasant).
7 malo (bad).
8 cierto (certain).
9 rápido (fast).
10 claro (clear).

54 COMPARISON OF ADJECTIVES AND ADVERBS

The comparison of equality 'as ... as' is rendered by
tan ... como:

Carlos es tan alto como Pedro.
Carlos is as tall as Pedro.
Nadie habla tan despacio como Juan.
Nobody talks as slowly as Juan.

The comparison of inequality ('more ... than', 'less than') is rendered by **más ... que, menos ... que**:

Yo soy más pobre que Vd.
I am poorer than you.
María es menos inteligente que su hermana.
Maria is less intelligent than her sister.
Mi mujer ha llegado más tarde que yo.
My wife has arrived later than I.
Este hombre trabaja menos diligentemente que aquél.
This man works less diligently than that one.

55 IRREGULAR COMPARISON OF ADJECTIVES

bueno (good)→ **mejor** (better)
malo (bad)→ **peor** (worse)
mucho (a lot of)→ **más** (more)
poco (little, few)→ **menos** (less, fewer)
grande (big)→ **mayor** (bigger, older)
pequeño (small)→ **menor** (smaller, younger)

Grande and **pequeño** also have a regular comparison,
más grande and **más pequeño**, which refers only to size:

Esta casa es más grande que la mía.
This house is bigger than mine.

Mejor, **peor**, **mayor**, and **menor** have a plural form
ending in **-es**, for masculine and feminine.

56 IRREGULAR COMPARISON OF ADVERBS

bien (well)→ **mejor** (better)
mal (badly)→ **peor** (worse)
mucho (much)→ **más** (more)
poco (little)→ **menos** (less)

Pilar canta mal, pero yo canto peor que ella.
Pilar sings badly, but I sing worse than she does.

57 COMPARISON OF NOUNS

The comparison of inequality has the same forms as that of adjectives and adverbs: **más ... que, menos ... que**:

Carmen tiene más paciencia que Pilar.
Carmen has more patience than Pilar.
Tengo menos libros que tú.
I have fewer books than you.

The comparison of equality is expressed by **tanto ... como**. As **tanto** is an adjective, it has to agree in gender and number with the following noun:

No he bebido tanto vino como Pedro.
I haven't drunk as much wine as Pedro.
Vd. no recibe tantas cartas como yo.
You don't receive as many letters as I do.

VOCABULARY	
fuerte	strong
el jerez	sherry
seco	dry
negro	black
el zapato	shoe
azul	blue
pronto	soon
necesitar	to need
el agua (f.)	water
caliente	hot, warm
la piscina	swimming pool

7

Exercise 31

Translate:

1 My brother is stronger than I.
2 This sherry is drier than that one.
3 Carlos is three years older than María.
4 The black shoes are smaller than the blue (ones).
5 His car is better than mine.
6 He writes worse than his sister.
7 I have arrived sooner than my father.
8 They haven't as much money as their friends.
9 I don't need as many suitcases as you.
10 The water in the pool is warmer than in the sea.

Drill 11

7

Example:
¿Iban Vds. al mercado? Did you go to the market?
Sí, solíamos ir. Yes, we used to go.
¿Leía Vd. el periódico? Did you read the paper?
Sí, solía leerlo. Yes, I used to read it.

1 ¿Veía Vd. a Carmen?
2 ¿Comían en el hotel?
3 ¿Trabajaban Vds.?
4 ¿Escribía Vd. cartas?
5 ¿Viajaba a Londres?
6 ¿Iban Vds. al café?
7 ¿Hablaba Vd. español?
8 ¿Invitaba a sus amigos?
9 ¿Tenían dinero?
10 ¿Bebía Vd. vino?

Drills 12-13

Example:
¿Ha venido alguien? Has anyone come?
No, no ha venido nadie. No, nobody has come.

1 ¿Quiere Vd. algo?
2 ¿Han vivido aquí siempre?
3 ¿Quieren Vds. té o café?
4 ¿Hay algún turista inglés?
5 ¿Conocen Vds. a alguien?
6 ¿Tiene Vd. alguna revista española?

Example:
Mi casa es pequeña. My house is small.
La mía es más pequeña. Mine is smaller.

1 Mis libros son viejos.
2 Mi coche es malo.
3 Mi jardín es bonito.
4 Mi hotel es bueno.
5 Mi marido es alto.
6 Mis zapatos son caros.
7 Mis maletas son grandes.
8 Mis cigarrillos son baratos.

7

El Sr. Sánchez habla con su secretaria

SR. SÁNCHEZ **Buenos días, Lolita. Llego más tarde que de costumbre.**

LOLITA **Sí. ¿Qué le ha ocurrido? Son casi las diez.**

SR. SÁNCHEZ **El coche no arrancaba esta mañana. Como ha helado durante la noche, el motor estaba muy frío.**

LOLITA **¡Qué lata! Por eso yo nunca vengo en el coche. Uso el Metro. Es mucho más rápido y me ahorro muchos problemas.**

SR. SÁNCHEZ **Claro. Así no tiene Vd. gastos ni de gasolina ni de aparcamiento. Yo creo que voy a hacer lo mismo pronto.**

LOLITA **Es lo mejor. No lo dude.**

SR. SÁNCHEZ **¿Ha venido alguien?**

LOLITA **No. No ha venido nadie.**

SR. SÁNCHEZ **Y, ¿hay algún recado?**

LOLITA **No, nada. Hay algunas cartas que he dejado en su escritorio.**

SR. SÁNCHEZ **Bueno. Entonces, voy a ver el correo, y dentro de media hora venga Vd. a mi despacho porque quiero dictarle unas cartas.**

LOLITA **Muy bien, Sr. Sánchez.**

TRANSLATION

Mr. Sánchez speaks with his secretary

MR. SÁNCHEZ Good morning, Lolita. I'm later than usual.
LOLITA Yes. What's happened to you? It's almost ten o'clock.
MR. SÁNCHEZ The car wouldn't start this morning. As it has been freezing during the night, the engine was very cold.
LOLITA What a nuisance! That is why I never come in the car. I use the Underground. It's much quicker and I save myself a lot of problems.
MR. SÁNCHEZ Of course. That way you have no expenses of either petrol or parking. I think I am going to do the same soon.
LOLITA It's the best thing. Believe me.
MR. SÁNCHEZ Has anyone called?
LOLITA No. Nobody has called.
MR. SÁNCHEZ And are there any messages?
LOLITA No, nothing. There are some letters that I have left on your desk.
MR. SÁNCHEZ All right. I'm going to see the post, then; and in half an hour come to my office, because I want to dictate a few letters.
LOLITA Very well, Mr. Sánchez.

7

Drill 1

Work through this drill in exactly the same way as all the others you have done so far.

¿Qué prefieres, el té o el café?
What do you prefer, tea or coffee?

Me gusta más el café.
I like coffee better/I prefer coffee.

1 ¿Qué prefieren ustedes, el vino o la cerveza?
   … el vino.

2 ¿Qué preferís, la carne o el pescado?
   … la carne.

3 ¿Qué prefiere Carlos, el campo o la playa?
   … la playa.

4 ¿Qué prefieres, el fútbol o el rugby?
   … el rugby.

5 ¿Qué prefieren los niños, jugar o ver la televisión?
   … jugar.

6 ¿Qué prefiere usted, Barcelona o Madrid?
   … Barcelona.

Exercise 1

Translate: ·

1 I am going to a party tomorrow and I need a new dress.

2 We have seen a very good film at the 'Roxy'.

3 He cannot come to the beach with us, he's got too much work.

4 Pedro is very pleasant, but he has no patience with the children.

5 The performance doesn't start till 10.15 p.m. – it's too late for us.

6 They have not been able to go out because it has rained all day.

7 We have to wait until 4.30 p.m. because the shops are closed (cerradas).

Drill 2

Practise your imperatives!

¿Compro el pan? Shall I buy the bread?

Sí, cómprelo. Yes, buy it.

No, no lo compre. No, don't buy it.

1 ¿Lavo este vestido?
   Sí, ...

2 ¿Espero a Carmen?
   No, ...

3 ¿Pregunto a ese señor?
   Sí, ...

4 ¿Me llevo las tazas?
   No, ...

5 ¿Llamo al gerente?
   Sí, ...

6 ¿Invito a Miguel?
   No, ...

7 ¿Pongo las flores en agua?
   Sí, ...

8 ¿Hago el café?
   No, ...

When you've done this drill, answering 'Sí' or 'No' as indicated, you could work through it again and reverse your replies ... you won't find these alternatives in the Key, but it's all useful extra practice.

Drill 3

More imperatives!

¿Compramos el pan? Shall we buy the bread?

Sí, cómprenlo. Yes, buy it.

No, no lo compren. No, don't buy it.

1 ¿Terminamos el vino?
  Sí, ...

2 ¿Pedimos el pescado?
  No, ...

3 ¿Vemos la habitación?
  Sí, ...

4 ¿Nos bañamos en la piscina?
  No, ...

5 ¿Compramos unos periódicos?
  Sí, ...

6 ¿Preparamos la cena?
  No, ...

7 ¿Enviamos las cartas?
  Sí, ...

8 ¿Ayudamos a Pedro?
  Sí, ...

7

Exercise 2

Complete the sentences given in column A with the correct sentence from column B:

A   B

1 Juan está en el hospital ...   a) el agua estaba fría.
2 Queremos ir al cine ...   b) hay demasiados
                                              turistas.
3 Vienen todos los años a   c) ha ido a llamar
   España ...   por teléfono.
4 El viernes es su   d) se ha roto una
   cumpleaños ...   pierna.
5 Estoy esperando a mi   e) si queremos
   marido...   comprar todos
                                              esos regalos.
6 No han querido bañarse   f) les gusta mucho
   en la piscina ...   el sol.
7 Vamos a necesitar más   g) ponen una película
   dinero ...   muy buena.
8 No me gustan los pueblos   h) va a dar una fiesta
   de la costa ...   en su casa.

Exercise 3

Here is a conversation between you and María about your friend Luisa's birthday. Put your words into Spanish.

USTED The day after tomorrow is Luisa's birthday.
MARÍA Sí, tenemos que comprarle un regalo.
USTED What can we buy her?
MARÍA No sé, ¿tienes alguna idea?
USTED I can only think of chocolates, flowers ....
MARÍA No, no. Tiene que ser algo más original.
USTED She reads a lot and she likes travelling.
       Why don't we buy her a travel book (libro
       de viajes)?
MARÍA Bueno, eso es una posibilidad.
USTED Then, we go shopping this afternoon and we
       look for something.
MARÍA ¡Vale!

Week 8

- shortened forms of adjectives
- adjectives which always precede the noun
- three irregular present tenses and some irregular past participles
- the future tense ('I will/shall do')
- the conditional tense ('I would do')
- verbs preceded by prepositions
- idioms using 'llevar' ('to wear', 'to carry') and 'hacer' ('to do', 'to make')

58 SHORTENING OF ADJECTIVES

The following adjectives have shortened forms:

1 before the masculine noun

bueno (good)	**buen**
malo (bad)	**mal**
alguno (some)	**algún**
ninguno (none)	**ningún**
primero (first)	**primer**
tercero (third)	**tercer**
uno (one)	**un**

2 before nouns of either gender

grande (big)	**gran**
ciento (100)	**cien**
cualquiera (any)	**cualquier**

Un buen libro   A good book
Una buena película   A good film
El primer tren   The first train
La primera fila   The first row
Cualquier autobús   Any bus
Cualquier persona   Any person

59 ADJECTIVES WHICH PRECEDE THE NOUN

Adjectives in Spanish usually follow the noun, but there are some exceptions. Adjectives which always precede the noun are:

1 adjectives of quantity

mucho	a lot of
poco	little
tanto	so much
cuanto	how much
demasiado	too much
bastante	enough

2 indefinite adjectives

alguno	some, any
ninguno	none
cada	each
otro	other
todo	all
tal	such

cada is an invariable word:

Cada hombre y cada mujer
Each man and each woman

otro is never preceded by the indefinite article:

Otro hombre y otra mujer
Another man and another woman

tal is invariable and never followed by the indefinite article:

Tal hombre y tal mujer
Such a man and such a woman

3 numerals (cardinal and ordinal) – but see section 25 for exceptions.

8

4 Some common adjectives like **bueno** (good), **malo** (bad), **pequeño** (small), **hermoso** (beautiful), **joven** (young), and **viejo** (old) often precede the noun:

Un hermoso paisaje A beautiful landscape
Un joven guitarrista A young guitarist

Certain adjectives change their meaning according to their position:

grande
Una casa grande A big house
but
Una gran mujer A great (famous) woman

nuevo
Un coche nuevo A (brand) new car
but
Un nuevo coche A new (different) car

pobre
Un hombre pobre A poor (impecunious) man
but
Un pobre hombre An unfortunate man

mismo
El mismo hombre The same man
but
El hombre mismo The man himself

In spite of all these rules, the position of adjectives in Spanish is fairly flexible and is often determined by emphasis, balance, and style; observation and practice will help the student to overcome any initial difficulties.

8

VOCABULARY

el pintor	painter
llevar	to wear, to carry
la ropa	clothes
la zona	area
perder (ie)	to lose
el bolso	handbag
el sombrero	hat
la bebida	drink
el sello	postage stamp
el nadador	swimmer

Exercise 32

Translate:

1 We have had a good journey.
2 Each man had a job.
3 He is a great painter.
4 They always wear the same clothes.
5 There are enough hotels in this area.
6 The poor woman has lost her handbag.
7 I have a brand new hat.
8 We have asked for another drink.
9 These stamps are very old.
10 All the children are good swimmers.

60 PRESENT TENSE OF THREE IRREGULAR VERBS

venir	**oír**	**decir**
to come	to hear	to say, to tell
vengo	**oigo**	**digo**
vienes	**oyes**	**dices**
viene	**oye**	**dice**
venimos	**oímos**	**decimos**
venís	**oís**	**decís**
vienen	**oyen**	**dicen**

61 SOME IRREGULAR PAST PARTICIPLES

abrir (to open)→ **abierto**
decir (to say)→ **dicho**
poner (to put)→ **puesto**
romper (to break)→ **roto**
volver (to return)→ **vuelto**
describir (to describe)→ **descrito**

(See section 32 for others)

62 THE FUTURE TENSE ('I WILL/SHALL DO')

The future tense of regular verbs is formed by adding
the following endings to the infinitive: **-é, -ás, -á,
-emos, -éis, -án**.

hablar	**comer**	**vivir**
to speak	to eat	to live
hablaré	**comeré**	**viviré**
hablarás	**comerás**	**vivirás**
hablará	**comerá**	**vivirá**
hablaremos	**comeremos**	**viviremos**
hablaréis	**comeréis**	**viviréis**
hablarán	**comerán**	**vivirán**

Hablaremos en español todo el tiempo.
We shall speak Spanish all the time.
Comerá con nosotros mañana.
He will eat with us tomorrow.
Vivirán cerca de sus padres.
They will live near his parents.

63 IRREGULAR VERBS IN THE FUTURE TENSE

A few verbs are irregular in the future tense. The endings remain the same as for regular verbs, but the stem changes:

caber (to fit in)	**cabré, cabrás, etc**
decir (to say)	**diré, dirás, etc**
haber (to have)	**habré, habrás, etc**
hacer (to do)	**haré, harás, etc**
poder (to be able)	**podré, podrás, etc**
poner (to put)	**pondré, pondrás, etc**
querer (to want)	**querré, querrás, etc**
saber (to know)	**sabré, sabrás, etc**
salir (to go out)	**saldré, saldrás, etc**
tener (to have)	**tendré, tendrás, etc**
valer (to be worth)	**valdré, valdrás, etc**
venir (to come)	**vendré, vendrás, etc**

No podremos ir. We shall not be able to go.
Diré unas pocas palabras. I shall say a few words.
Vendrán con él. They will come with him.

64 THE CONDITIONAL TENSE ('I WOULD DO')

The conditional is formed by adding to the infinitive the following endings: **-ía, -ías, -ía, -íamos, -íais, -ían.**

hablar	**comer**	**vivir**
hablaría	**comería**	**viviría**
hablarías	**comerías**	**vivirías**
hablaría	**comería**	**viviría**
hablaríamos	**comeríamos**	**viviríamos**
hablaríais	**comeríais**	**viviríais**
hablarían	**comerían**	**vivirían**

As the first and third persons singular have the same forms, the subject pronoun is sometimes used in order to avoid ambiguity:

8

Me gustaría ir a la fiesta.
I should like to go to the party.
No vivirían en España.
They would not live in Spain.

65 IRREGULAR VERBS IN THE CONDITIONAL

Verbs which are irregular in the future tense are also
irregular in the conditional with the same stem change:

**decir→ diría; hacer→ haría; tener→ tendría;
venir→ vendría**, etc

Yo quería saber lo que diría.
I wanted to know what he would say.
Tendrían que pagar el daño.
They would have to pay the damage.

66 USES OF THE FUTURE AND CONDITIONAL

There are substantial differences between the use of the
future and conditional in English and in Spanish, where the
tenses may be used to express probability or assumption:

¿Por qué no ha venido Pedro?
Why hasn't Pedro come?
Estará enfermo.
He is probably ill.
¿Cuántos años tenía el niño?
How old was the boy?
Tendría nueve años.
He must have been nine.

The English 'will' and 'would' expressing will or
determination are translated by **querer**:

No quiere contestar el teléfono.
He will not answer the phone.

No quería venir con nosotros.
He would not come with us.
¿Quiere Vd. un café?
Will you have a coffee?
¿Quiere Vd. cerrar la puerta, por favor?
Will you shut the door, please?

'Shall' introducing a suggestion, as in the following examples, is translated by the present tense:

¿Nos sentamos?
Shall we sit down?
¿Llamo a la policía?
Shall I call the police?

'Should' introducing an obligation or recommendation is translated by the conditional form of **deber**:

Deberías decirles la verdad.
You should tell them the truth.
Miguel debería dejar de fumar.
Michael should give up smoking.

8

VOCABULARY

próximo	next
temprano	early
esta noche	tonight
conducir	to drive
andar	to walk
lejos	far
el museo	museum
el autocar	coach

Translate:

1 They will get married next month.
2 I shall go to bed early tonight.
3 He will come with us on holiday.
4 We shall visit them on Sunday.
5 They will not speak to us.
6 It would be better to stop.
7 I shouldn't like to drive a big car.
8 He won't have to walk very far.
9 They wouldn't be worth anything.
10 We shan't be able to see the museum.
11 He would not sell the house.
12 The coach will leave at eight o'clock.

67 VERBS WITH PREPOSITIONS

8

A verb that is preceded by a preposition must always be an infinitive:

Le veré antes de salir.
I'll see him before leaving.
Se ha ido sin hablar con nosotros.
He has left without speaking to us.

VOCABULARY

cerrar (ie)	to close
la ventana	window
antes de	before
después de	after
de	of, from
pasar	to spend (time)
llorar	to cry
sentirse (ie)	to feel
enfermo	ill
el marisco	seafood
la habitación	room
tomar	to take
la voz	voice
ronco (-a)	hoarse
gritar	to shout
enseñar	to show

Exercise 34

Translate:

1 Close the windows before going to bed.
2 I shall have to think before deciding.
3 You cannot go without finishing the job.
4 He has spent the day without speaking to anyone.
5 She was crying without knowing why.
6 They were feeling ill after eating seafood.
7 I was very sleepy after working all night.
8 We should like to see the room before taking it.
9 His voice was hoarse from shouting so much.
10 After writing the letter show it to me.

8

Llevar (to wear, to carry) and **hacer** (to do, to make) are often used to express how long an action has or had been going on:

¿Cuánto tiempo lleva Vd. en España?
How long have you been in Spain?
Hace tres meses que estoy aquí.
I have been here three months.
¿Cuánto tiempo llevan Vds. esperando?
How long have you been waiting?
Hace media hora que esperamos.
We have been waiting half an hour.

Question and answer can be reversed thus:

¿Cuánto tiempo hace que está Vd. en España?
Llevo tres meses aquí.

¿Cuánto tiempo hace que esperan Vds?
Llevamos media hora esperando.

8

Drills 14–15

Example:
¿Ha venido tu amigo? Has your friend come?
No, vendrá luego. No, he will come later.
¿Ha leído Vd. el periódico? Have you read the newspaper?
No, lo leeré luego. No, I shall read it later.

1 ¿Han visto a su padre?
2 ¿Han terminado Vds. el trabajo?
3 ¿Ha ido Vd. al banco?
4 ¿Ha escrito Pedro la carta?
5 ¿Han enviado Vds. las flores?
6 ¿Han cerrado la tienda?
7 ¿Ha salido Juan?
8 ¿Ha hecho Vd. la comida?
9 ¿Han visto las habitaciones?
10 ¿Ha abierto Vd. las ventanas?

Study the examples in section 68, then do the following drill:

1 ¿Cuánto tiempo lleva Vd. estudiando español?
… seis meses ….
2 ¿Cuánto tiempo llevan Vds. en Madrid?
… tres años ….
3 ¿Cuánto tiempo llevan ellos trabajando aquí?
… dos semanas ….
4 ¿Cuánto tiempo lleva Juan viviendo en Los Angeles?
… un año ….
5 ¿Cuánto tiempo lleva Vd. esperando?
… diez minutos ….
6 ¿Cuánto tiempo hace que estudia Vd. español?
… seis meses ….
7 ¿Cuánto tiempo hace que están Vds. en Madrid?
… tres años ….
8 ¿Cuánto tiempo hace que ellos trabajan aquí?
… dos semanas ….
9 ¿Cuánto tiempo hace que Juan vive en Los Angeles?
… un año ….
10 ¿Cuánto tiempo hace que espera Vd.?
… diez minutos ….

8

CONVERSATION

Un encuentro en la calle

PEDRO **Teresa, ¡cuánto tiempo sin vernos!**

TERESA **¿Cómo estás?**

PEDRO **Muy bien, gracias. Y tú ¿qué haces en Madrid? ¿No vivías en Sevilla?**

TERESA **Ya no. Mi marido está trabajando aquí ahora. Llevamos tres meses en Madrid.**

PEDRO **¡Ah, muy bien! ¿Habéis encontrado piso ya?**

TERESA **No. De momento estamos viviendo con los padres de Antonio. Pero el piso no es muy grande y estamos un poco apretados.**

PEDRO **¿Qué tipo de piso buscáis? Porque tengo un amigo que vende uno con tres dormitorios, salón, comedor, cocina y baño. Y también tiene una terraza bastante grande. Lo que no sé es lo que pide. ¿Crees que puede interesarte?**

TERESA **¡Ya lo creo! Si el precio es razonable. ¿Cómo podemos ponernos en contacto con él?**

PEDRO **Se llama Alberto Solís, y estos son su teléfono y sus señas.**

TERESA **Pues, muchísimas gracias, Pedro. A ver si tenemos suerte.**

PEDRO **Eso espero. Hasta pronto.**

TERESA **Sí. Te llamaremos. Adiós.**

8

120 | SPANISH IN THREE MONTHS

A chance meeting in the street

PEDRO Teresa, we haven't met for a long time!

TERESA How are you?

PEDRO Very well, thank you. And you, what are you doing in Madrid? Weren't you living in Seville?

TERESA No longer. My husband is working here now. We have been in Madrid three months.

PEDRO Oh, very good! Have you found a flat yet?

TERESA No. At the moment we are living with Antonio's parents. But the flat is not very big and we are a little cramped.

PEDRO What sort of flat are you looking for? Because I have a friend who is selling one with three bedrooms, lounge, dining room, kitchen and bathroom. It also has quite a large balcony. What I don't know is how much he is asking. Do you think it may interest you?

TERESA Yes, indeed! If the price is reasonable. How can we get in touch with him?

PEDRO His name is Alberto Solís, and this is his phone number and address.

TERESA Well, thank you very much, Pedro. Let's see if we are lucky.

PEDRO I hope so. See you soon.

TERESA Yes. We'll call you. 'Bye.

8

Week 9

- the past historic tense, ('I spoke', 'I ate') in regular and irregular verbs
- when to use the past historic and when to use the imperfect
- the difference between 'saber' and 'conocer' (both meaning 'to know')
- the superlative of adjectives and adverbs ('poorest,' 'biggest')
- uses of the neuter article 'lo'
- other uses of the definite and indefinite articles

69 THE PAST HISTORIC ('I SPOKE', 'I ATE')

The past historic is used to express a completed action, an action that took place within a definite period of time.

hablar	comer	vivir
hablé	comí	viví
hablaste	comiste	viviste
habló	comió	vivió
hablamos	comimos	vivimos
hablasteis	comisteis	vivisteis
hablaron	comieron	vivieron

Ayer hablé con Carmen.
Yesterday I spoke to Carmen.
Comieron sopa y pescado.
They ate soup and fish.
Vivió en Madrid diez años.
He lived in Madrid ten years.

There is an important group of verbs which are irregular in the past historic (sometimes called the past definite). The endings are the same for all of them but the stem changes. Here are three examples:

andar	hacer	venir
to walk	to do/make	to come
anduve	hice	vine
anduviste	hiciste	viniste
anduvo	hizo	vino
anduvimos	hicimos	vinimos
anduvisteis	hicisteis	vinisteis
anduvieron	hicieron	vinieron

Other verbs belonging to the same group are listed below, with their first person singular past historic form:

estar (to be)	estuve
decir (to say)	dije
saber (to know)	supe
poner (to put)	puse
poder (to be able)	pude
conducir (to drive)	conduje
querer (to want)	quise
haber (to have)	hube
tener (to have)	tuve
traer (to bring)	traje

No quiso abrir la puerta.
He didn't want to open the door.
Estuve enfermo dos meses.
I was ill for two months.
No pudieron venir juntos.
They weren't able to come together.

Note that the third person plural of **decir, conducir, traer** is **dijeron, condujeron, trajeron** (the **i** of the ending is omitted after the **j**).

71 PAST HISTORIC OF 'SER' AND 'IR'

Ser and **ir** both have the same irregular form in the past historic:

fui	**fuimos**
fuiste	**fuisteis**
fue	**fueron**

El verano pasado fui a Mallorca.
Last summer I went to Mallorca.
Fue un hombre muy famoso.
He was a very famous man.

72 PAST HISTORIC OF 'DAR' (TO GIVE)

di	**dimos**
diste	**disteis**
dio	**dieron**

Me dio un recado para Vd.
He gave me a message for you.
Les di veinte euros.
I gave them twenty euros.

9

73 STEM-CHANGING VERBS: PAST HISTORIC

There is a small group of verbs ending in **-ir** which are irregular in the third persons (singular and plural) of the past historic. The '**e**' in the stem becomes '**i**' and the '**o**' becomes '**u**'. The rest of the tense is regular:

	3rd pers. sing.	3rd pers. pl.
seguir (to follow)	**siguió**	**siguieron**
pedir (to ask for)	**pidió**	**pidieron**
sentir (to feel)	**sintió**	**sintieron**
dormir (to sleep)	**durmió**	**durmieron**
morir (to die)	**murió**	**murieron**

Durmió solamente cuatro horas.
He slept only four hours.
Pidieron dos botellas de vino.
They asked for two bottles of wine.

VOCABULARY

dar un paseo	to go for a walk
por	along
el río	river
el sobre	envelope
pagar	to pay
la comida	meal
el cheque	cheque
el camarero	waiter
el kilómetro	kilometre
la hora de comer	lunch time

Exercise 35

Translate:

1 We went for a walk along the river.

2 They didn't want to see me.

3 I put the letter in the envelope.

4 He died two years later.

5 He paid for the meal with a cheque.

6 The waiter brought us the drinks and went away.

7 They walked five kilometres looking for a garage.

8 I went out at ten o'clock and returned at lunch time.

9 We told him that his father had arrived.

10 He didn't do anything all morning.

9

It is sometimes difficult for the student to decide whether to use the imperfect or the past historic, since, at times, they can be both translated by the English 'did'. Remember that the imperfect tells us what was going on, what somebody was doing or used to do over an indefinite period of time, whereas the past historic expresses what happened or what somebody did at a particular time. Study the following examples:

Nadábamos en el río todos los días.
We swam (used to swim) in the river every day.
Ayer nadamos en el río.
Yesterday we swam in the river.
Siempre fumaba un puro después de cenar.
He always smoked (used to smoke) a cigar after dinner.
Anoche fumó un puro después de cenar.
Last night he smoked a cigar after dinner.
Llovía cuando salimos del hotel.
It was raining when we left the hotel.
Llovió toda la tarde.
It rained all afternoon.

9

VOCABULARY

la ducha	shower
sonar (ue)	to sound, to ring
jugar (ue)	to play
mientras	while
bajar	to go down
la cuenta	bill
hacer la maleta	to pack
cansado (-a)	tired
la (tarjeta) postal	postcard
el policía	policeman
preguntar	to ask

Exercise 36

Change the infinitives in brackets into the correct form of the imperfect or past historic as appropriate.

1 Aquella mañana Ramón (salir) de su casa a las nueve.

2 Yo (estar) en la ducha cuando (sonar) el teléfono.

3 Cuando Carmen y María (viajar) a Valencia (tener) un accidente.

4 Los niños (jugar) en el jardín cuando (empezar) a llover.

5 Juan (bajar) a pagar la cuenta, mientras yo (hacer) la maleta.

6 Mi padre siempre (sentarse) en el mismo sillón.

7 Yo (volver) a casa muy cansada.

8 (Hacer) frío cuando nosotros (llegar) a Bilbao.

9 Luis (recibir) una postal de un amigo que (vivir) en Londres.

10 El policía me (preguntar) mi nombre y dirección.

75 THE TWO VERBS 'TO KNOW'

It is important to differentiate between the verbs **saber** and **conocer**, both meaning 'to know'. **Saber** is to know a fact. **Conocer** is 'to be acquainted with'. For example:

No sabemos cuando llegará.
We don't know when he will arrive.
Sé que está enfermo.
I know that he is ill.
Conocemos a tu hermana muy bien.
We know your sister very well.
No conozco* esa ciudad.
I don't know that town.

*The verb **conocer** and a few others ending in **-cer** and **-cir** preceded by a vowel take a **z** before the **c** in the first person of the present indicative. The rest of the tense is regular.

9

conocer (to know)→ **conozco** (I know)
obedecer (to obey)→ **obedezco** (I obey)
pertenecer (to belong)→ **pertenezco** (I belong)
conducir (to drive)→ **conduzco** (I drive)
traducir (to translate)→ **traduzco** (I translate)

76   SUPERLATIVE OF ADJECTIVES ('BIGGEST')

The superlative is formed by putting **el más, la más, los más, las más** in front of the adjective.

For example:
Este hombre es el más pobre del pueblo.
This man is the poorest in the village.
Nuestra casa es la más grande de la calle.
Our house is the biggest in the street.

When the superlative immediately follows the noun, the article is omitted:

Es el edificio más alto de Madrid.
It is the highest building in Madrid.
Es la novela más interesante que he leído.
It is the most interesting novel I have read.

77   SUPERLATIVE OF ADVERBS

The superlative is formed by putting **lo más** in front of the adverb. (For more about **lo**, see section 79.)

Hágalo Vd. lo más pronto posible.
Do it as soon as possible.
Les escribiré el martes lo más tarde.
I'll write to them on Tuesday at the latest.

78 THE ABSOLUTE SUPERLATIVE

The ending **-ísimo** added to adjectives or adverbs renders the English 'most', 'extremely':

Es una mujer inteligentísima.
She is a most intelligent woman.
Es un libro aburridísimo.
It is an extremely boring book.
Llegaron al acropuerto tardísimo.
They arrived at the airport extremely late.
Hoy me he levantado tempranísimo.
Today I have got up extremely early.

VOCABULARY

el CD	CD
el ordenador	computer
el programa de televisión	television programme
divertido	amusing
la talla	size
amable	kind
interesante	interesting
la conversación	conversation
viejo	old
la farmacia	chemist's shop
la parada de autobús	bus stop

9

Translate:

1 They don't know that CD.

2 He knows that I want a computer.

3 That television programme is most amusing.

4 This size is the smallest we have.

5 These shoes are the prettiest, those are the cheapest.

6 He is the kindest man I know.

7 They don't know that I want to see them.

8 It was a most interesting conversation.

9 It is the oldest church in this town.

10 The chemist's was far from the bus stop.

79 USE OF THE NEUTER ARTICLE 'LO'

We have already seen examples of **lo** preceding:

1 an adverb

Contestó lo mejor que pudo.
He answered as best he could.

2 the relative **que**

Lo que quiero decir.
What I want to say.

But also **lo** may precede an adjective, thus turning it into an abstract noun:

Lo difícil es conseguir el dinero.
The difficult thing is to obtain the money.
Lo importante es llegar a tiempo.
The important thing is to arrive on time.

USES OF THE DEFINITE AND INDEFINITE
ARTICLES

The definite article is used in Spanish in the following
cases:

1 before nouns used in a general sense

El vino es barato en España.
Wine is cheap in Spain.

2 before abstract nouns

El amor es ciego.
Love is blind.

3 before titles

La reina Isabel de Inglaterra
Queen Elizabeth of England
El señor y la señora Ruiz/Los señores Ruiz
Mr. and Mrs. Ruiz

4 before names of institutions, public places, etc

el hospital (hospital), **la iglesia** (church),
la universidad (university)

5 before proper nouns qualified by an adjective

El pobre Carlos Poor Charles
El viejo Madrid Old Madrid

6 before parts of the body and articles of clothing, when
in English the possessive 'my', 'his', etc would be used

Se ha roto la pierna.
He has broken his leg.
Me pondré el abrigo azul.
I shall put on my blue coat.

7 before days of the week, seasons and certain expressions of time

Volveremos el martes. We shall return on Tuesday.
El invierno se acerca. Winter is approaching.
Le vi la semana pasada. I saw him last week.

8 in certain set expressions

El diez por ciento de rebaja Ten per cent reduction
Seis euros el kilo Six euros per kilo

The indefinite article is used before an abstract noun qualified by an adjective. For example:

Condujo a una velocidad increíble.
He drove at an incredible speed.

But it is not used:

1 before a noun indicating occupation, nationality, religion, or politics:

Es contable. He is an accountant.
Es española. She is Spanish.
Soy protestante. I am a protestant.
¿Es Vd. conservador? Are you a conservative?

However, if the noun is qualified by an adjective the article is used:

Es un buen contable. He is a good accountant.

2 before certain words:

otro (another), **cierto** (certain), **medio** (half a), **cien** (a hundred), **mil** (a thousand), **tal** (such a), **¡qué!** (what a!)

Voy a comprar otro periódico.
I am going to buy another newspaper.

Cierta mujer que conozco. A certain woman I know.
Medio litro de leche. Half a litre of milk.
¡Qué desastre! What a disaster!

VOCABULARY

ponerse	to put on
el guante	glove
la dependienta	shop assistant (f.)
principal	main
preocuparse	to worry
romper(se)	to break
derecho	right
el brazo	arm
hoy día	nowadays
la dificultad	difficulty
la botella	bottle
el coñac	brandy

Exercise 38

Translate:

1 Tea is a very pleasant drink.
2 Mrs Collado will arrive on Sunday.
3 She put on her gloves because it was cold.
4 He is a waiter and she is a shop assistant.
5 I spent two weeks in hospital.
6 The main thing is not to worry.
7 Poor Mary has broken her right arm.
8 Books are very expensive nowadays.
9 He used to walk with great difficulty.
10 He is going to bring another cup.
11 We drank half a bottle of brandy.
12 The best thing is to sell the house.

9

Example:
Yo no quería invitar a Carmen . . . pero tuve que invitarla.
I didn't want to invite Carmen . . . but I had to invite her.
Nosotros no queríamos ir a la playa . . . pero tuvimos que ir.
We didn't want to go to the beach . . . but we had to go.

1 Pedro no quería escribir la carta . . .
2 Ellos no querían pagar la cuenta . . .
3 Yo no quería ver a Juan . . .
4 Nosotros no queríamos ir a la fiesta . . .
5 Vd. no quería salir del hotel . . .
6 Carmen no quería hacer la comida . . .
7 El niño no quería comer el pescado . . .
8 María no quería fumar un cigarrillo . . .
9 Yo no quería darle mi nombre . . .
10 Nosotros no queríamos beber la cerveza . . .

Example:
¿Has hablado con Pedro hoy? Have you spoken with Pedro today?
No, hablé ayer. No, I spoke yesterday.
¿Han visto Vds. a Conchita hoy? Have you seen Conchita today?
No, la vimos ayer. No, we saw her yesterday.

1 ¿Han estado Vds. en la playa hoy?
2 ¿Han venido tus padres hoy?
3 ¿Ha comprado Vd. este libro hoy?
4 ¿Han pagado la cuenta hoy?
5 ¿Ha recibido Juan la postal hoy?
6 ¿Han hecho Vds. las maletas hoy?
7 ¿Ha llovido hoy?
8 ¿Han traído las flores hoy?
9 ¿Han ido Vds. al museo hoy?
10 ¿Ha visitado Vd. a sus amigos hoy?

9

Drill 18

Example:
Es una catedral muy grande. It's a very large cathedral.
Sí, es la más grande que he visto. Yes, it's the largest
I've seen.

1 Es un vestido muy bonito.
2 Son unos libros muy caros.
3 Es una playa muy grande.
4 Es un hotel muy elegante.
5 Son unos programas muy divertidos.
6 Son unas ventanas muy pequeñas.

9

Juan y Paloma hablan de lo que han hecho durante el fin de semana

JUAN   El sábado me levanté muy tarde porque estaba cansadísimo de trabajar tanto durante la semana.

PALOMA   ¿A qué le llamas tú tarde?

JUAN   A las doce y media o la una. Era casi la hora de comer. Mi mujer no estaba muy contenta porque quería ir de compras conmigo por la mañana.

PALOMA   Así que tuviste que ir por la tarde.

JUAN   Claro. Y fue larguísimo porque las tiendas estaban llenas de gente. Así que cuando volvimos, mi mujer preparó una cena rápida y nos sentamos a ver la televisión hasta las once y media.

PALOMA   Yo fui a una boda el sábado. Se casaba un primo mío.

JUAN   ¿Te divertiste?

PALOMA   Sí, estuvo muy bien. La comida fue buenísima, y la bebida también, claro. Hubo música y baile hasta las tres de la mañana.

JUAN   Y el domingo ¿qué hiciste?

PALOMA   Nada importante. Dormir, leer el periódico y ver la televisión ¿Y tú?

JUAN   Poco más o menos, lo mismo que tú.

9

TRANSLATION

Juan and Paloma talk about what they have done during the weekend

JUAN   On Saturday I got up very late because I was exhausted after working so hard during the week.

PALOMA   What do you call late?

JUAN   Half past twelve or one o'clock. It was almost lunch time. My wife wasn't very pleased because she wanted to go shopping with me in the morning.

PALOMA   So you had to go in the afternoon.

JUAN   Of course. And it was endless, because the shops were crowded. So, when we got back, my wife prepared a quick supper and we sat down to watch television until half past eleven.

PALOMA   I went to a wedding on Saturday. A cousin of mine was getting married.

JUAN   Did you have a good time?

PALOMA   Yes, it was fine. The food was very good and the drink too, of course. There was music and dancing till three in the morning.

JUAN   And Sunday, what did you do?

PALOMA   Nothing important. Sleep, read the paper and watch television. And you?

JUAN   More or less the same as you.

9

Week 10

- *the different uses of 'por' and 'para', both meaning 'for'*
- *the passive voice – how to form it, and how to avoid using it*
- *more spelling changes in verbs, to preserve the original pronunciation*
- *which verbs are followed directly by an infinitive, and which take a preposition before the infinitive*

81 DIFFERENT USES OF 'POR' AND 'PARA'

It is important to learn the uses of **por** and **para**, particularly as either word may translate the English 'for'.

Por is used to indicate means, motive, exchange. It translates the English: by, through, because of, out of, for the sake of, for:

Le di las gracias por las flores.
I thanked him for the flowers.
El ladrón entró por la ventana.
The thief came in through the window.
Lo hizo por nosotros.
He did it for us.
Envié el equipaje por tren.
I sent the luggage by train.

Para is used to indicate purpose, suitability or destination. It translates the English: for, to, in order to, so as to:

Necesito dinero para comprar los billetes.
I need money to buy the tickets.
Este abrigo es demasiado grande para mí.
This coat is too big for me.
El tren sale para Málaga dentro de cinco minutos.
The train leaves for Malaga within five minutes.
Es un regalo para Vd.
It is a present for you.

There are also many idiomatic uses of **por** and **para** which the student will learn by observation. Here are some examples:

Estamos para salir.
We are about to go out.
Estoy por no hacerlo.
I am inclined not to do it.
Lo dejaremos para mañana.
We shall leave it for tomorrow.
Una vez por semana Once a week
Por la tarde In the afternoon (evening)
Por ejemplo For example
Por último Finally
Por consiguiente Therefore, consequently
Por lo visto Evidently

VOCABULARY

joven	young
el sacrificio	sacrifice
pasar	to pass
la Aduana	Customs
cobrar	to charge
el cine	cinema
las compras	purchases, shopping
la llave	key
el armario	cupboard, wardrobe
difícil	difficult
el avión	aeroplane
cualquier cosa	anything
la curiosidad	curiosity
el melocotón	peach

10

Exercise 39

Fill in the gaps with 'por' or 'para' as appropriate:

1 Pagó seiscientos euros … el coche.
2 No podemos salir … esa puerta.
3 Voy de vacaciones … descansar.
4 Le llamaré … teléfono mañana.
5 Estas cartas no son … mí.
6 Es demasiado joven … comprenderlo.
7 Hizo ese sacrificio … su padre.
8 Hay que tener mucho dinero … viajar.
9 Saldremos …. Valencia el martes.
10 No pudo venir a la fiesta … estar enfermo.

Exercise 40

Translate:

1 We have to pass through the Customs.
2 They charged us ten euros for the meal.
3 It is too late to go to the cinema.
4 I need a bag for all my shopping.
5 Have you (pol.) a key to open this cupboard?
6 This book is too difficult for him.
7 The plane leaves for Madrid at a quarter past seven.
8 I would do anything for him.
9 We read the letter out of curiosity.
10 She wants to buy some peaches for her mother.

10

82 FORMING THE PASSIVE

The passive is formed with the verb **ser** followed by the past participle. The agent is usually introduced by **por**, although **de** is sometimes used after verbs of feeling and in some set expressions such as **cubierto de** (covered by) and **acompañado de** (accompanied by). In the passive the past participle agrees in gender and number with the subject.

La carta fue firmada por el presidente.
The letter was signed by the president.
El soldado fue herido por una bala.
The soldier was wounded by a bullet.

Note that the past participle is also used with **estar** to indicate state, whereas with **ser** it indicates action. Compare the following examples:

El libro está publicado en cinco idiomas.
The book is published in five languages.
El libro será publicado en cinco idiomas.
The book will be published in five languages.

83 AVOIDANCE OF THE PASSIVE

The passive is less frequently used in Spanish than in English, and is often avoided.

1 By using the reflexive pronoun **se**:

Se prohibe fumar.
Smoking is forbidden.
El museo se cierra a las seis.
The museum is closed at six.

se also translates the English 'one':

No se puede decir. One cannot tell.

10

2 By using the third person plural of the verb as an impersonal form:

Nos vieron salir de la casa.
They saw us (we were seen) leaving the house.
Dicen que no va a volver.
They say (it is said) that he is not coming back.

3 By changing the roles of subject and agent, using the active voice, so that 'she was shot by someone', for example, becomes 'someone shot her'. Thus:

Le paró la policía.
He was stopped by the police.

VOCABULARY	
construir	to build
el abuelo	grandfather
acusar	to accuse
el robo	theft
el barco	boat
ahora	now
creer	to believe
muerto	dead
la montaña	mountain
cubierto	covered
la nieve	snow
la cena	dinner
servir (i)	to serve
pintar	to paint
recibir	to receive
el director	director
presentar	to introduce
famoso	famous
el actor	actor

10

Exercise 41

Translate:

1 The house was built by his grandfather.
2 I was accused of the theft.
3 The boat was sold for five hundred euros.
4 The work is now finished.
5 It is believed that he is dead.
6 The mountains were covered in snow.
7 Dinner is not served until nine.
8 The windows were painted three weeks ago.
9 They were received by one of the directors.
10 The programme was introduced by a famous actor.

84 CHANGES OF SPELLING IN VERBS

Certain verbs have a change of spelling in the stem, in some parts of the conjugation, in order to preserve the original pronunciation. Verbs ending in:

-car change the **c** into **qu** before **e**:
buscar (to look for)→ **busqué** (I looked for)

-zar change the **z** into **c** before **e**:
empezar (to begin)→ **empecé** (I began)

-gar change the **g** into **gu** before **e**:
pagar (to pay)→ **pagué** (I paid)

-ger or **-gir** change the **g** into **j** before **a** or **o**:
coger (to pick up)→ **cojo** (I pick up)
dirigir (to direct)→ **dirija Vd.** (direct)

10

Note that an unaccented **i** between two vowels is always changed to **y**:

leer (to read)→ **leyó, leyeron** (he/they read)
creer (to think)→ **creyó, creyeron** (he/they thought)

huir (to flee)→ **huyó, huyeron** (he/they fled)
construir (to build)→ **construyó, construyeron**
 (he/they built)
oír (to hear)→ **oyó, oyeron** (he/they heard)
caer (to fall)→ **cayó, cayeron** (he/they fell)

These changes also occur in the present participle:

leyendo (reading)
creyendo (thinking)
huyendo (fleeing)
construyendo (building)
oyendo (hearing)
cayendo (falling)

VOCABULARY

el aparcamiento	car park
el ruido	noise
arriba	upstairs
secar(se)	to dry (oneself)
el pie	foot
al fuego	by the fire
el suelo	ground, floor
las instrucciones	instructions
el principio	beginning
la guerra	war
el cuadro	picture
el equipaje	luggage

10

Exercise 42

Translate:

1 I played with the children all afternoon.
2 They are building a new car park.
3 He heard a noise upstairs.
4 I dried my feet by the fire.
5 They fell to the ground.
6 He is reading the instructions.
7 They fled from Spain at the beginning of the war.
8 I paid a lot of money for that picture.
9 Pick up the luggage, please.
10 He thought that the shop was closed.

85   VERBS FOLLOWED BY AN INFINITIVE

Some Spanish verbs are directly followed by an infinitive, while others take a preposition before the infinitive. The following lists include some of the the most common verbs in each of these categories.

VERBS DIRECTLY FOLLOWED BY INFINITIVE

aconsejar (to advise)
Me aconsejó esperar. He advised me to wait.

conseguir (to manage to)
Conseguimos abrirlo. We managed to open it.

deber (must)
Debo visitarla más a menudo. I must visit her more often.

decidir (to decide)
Decidió venir conmigo. He decided to come with me.

esperar (to hope to)
Esperamos verle en España.
We hope to see him in Spain.

10

intentar (to try to)
Intenté encontrar un empleo. I tried to find a job.

parecer (to appear to, to seem)
Pareció ser una falsa alarma.
It appeared to be a false alarm.

pedir (to ask to)
Ha pedido hablar con el gerente.
He has asked to speak to the manager.

pensar (to intend)
Pienso salir muy temprano.
I intend to leave very early.

poder (to be able to, can)
No podíamos ver nada.
We could not see anything.

VERBS FOLLOWED BY A + INFINITIVE

entrar (to come in)
Entró a preguntar el precio.
He came in to ask the price.

empezar (to begin)
Empezó a comer. He began to eat.

enseñar (to teach)
Me enseñó a conducir. He taught me to drive.

aprender (to learn)
Aprendieron a nadar en seguida.
They quickly learned to swim.

decidirse (to decide)
Me decidí a decírselo. I decided to tell him.

volver (to return)
Volvió a recoger su maleta.
He came back to collect his suitcase.

Note that **volver a** can be used idiomatically with the meaning of 'to do something again':

Volví a verle al día siguiente.
I saw him again the following day.

VERBS FOLLOWED BY DE + INFINITIVE

acabar (to finish)
Acabó de leer la carta.
He finished reading the letter.

Note that **acabar de** used in the present or imperfect indicative has the meaning of 'to have just':

Acabo de ver a Juan. I have just seen John.
Acababan de salir. They had just gone out.

acordarse (to remember)
No se acordó de llevar su pasaporte.
He didn't remember to take his passport.

cansarse (to get tired)
Me cansé de andar. I got tired of walking.

dejar (to stop)
El niño dejó de llorar. The child stopped crying.

olvidarse (to forget)
Se olvidaron de comprar gasolina.
They forgot to buy petrol.

tratar (to try)
Traté de verle. I tried to see him.

VERBS FOLLOWED BY EN + INFINITIVE

consentir (to consent)
Ha consentido en hablar con ella.
He has consented to speak to her.

10

insistir (to insist)
Insistió en acompañarme. He insisted on going with me.

pensar (to think)
Pensaba en escribir a su amigo.
He was thinking of writing to his friend.

vacilar (to hesitate)
Vacilé en darle la noticia.
I hesitated to tell him the news.

tardar (to take time)
Tardó mucho en llegar. He took a long time to arrive.

VERBS FOLLOWED BY POR + INFINITIVE

acabar (to finish)
Acabé por darle el dinero.
I finished by giving him the money.

empezar (to begin)
Empezaremos por aprender el alfabeto.
We shall begin by learning the alphabet.

esforzarse (to make an effort)
Se esforzó por ser amable.
He made an effort to be kind.

VERBS FOLLOWED BY CON + INFINITIVE

amenazar (to threaten)
El hombre amenazó con disparar.
The man threatened to shoot.

soñar (to dream)
Sueña con hacer mucho dinero.
He dreams of making a lot of money.

contentarse (to content oneself)
Me contento con descansar unos minutos.
I content myself with resting for a few minutes.

VOCABULARY

alquilar	to hire
quejarse de	to complain
el servicio	service
jugar a	to play (a game)
el tenis	tennis
telefonear	to phone, to ring up
subir	to climb
el paquete	parcel
la discusión	argument
sonreír (i)	to smile
ganar	to earn

Exercise 43

Translate:

1 I managed to speak with them.

2 He advised us to hire a car.

3 They tried to come into the room.

4 I intend to complain about the service.

5 We are learning to play tennis.

6 I rang him up again.

7 Mr. Solís has just arrived.

8 He got tired of climbing and sat down.

9 It stopped raining and the sun came out.

10 I forgot to give him the message.

11 They insisted on paying for their tickets.

12 The parcel took two weeks to arrive.

13 They finished by having an argument.

14 The woman made an effort to smile.

15 The man threatened to call the police.

16 He contents himself with earning very little.

10

Drills 19–21

Fill in the blanks with either 'por' or 'para' as appropriate:

1 ¿Necesitas dinero? Sí, ... comprar los sellos.

2 ¿Ha comprado el vestido? Sí, ... treinta euros.

3 ¿Lleva Vd. un libro? Sí, ... leer en la playa.

4 ¿Has comprado un regalo? Sí, ... mi madre.

5 ¿Ha enviado Vd. el paquete? Sí, ... avión.

6 ¿Salen Vds. mañana? Sí, ... Inglaterra.

7 ¿Necesitas gafas? Sí, ... leer solamente.

8 ¿Han dado Vds. un paseo? Sí, ... el borde del río.

Avoid the passive voice by using the reflexive pronoun 'se':

El piso fue vendido. The flat was sold.
El piso se vendió. The flat was sold.

1 El libro fue publicado.

2 Los coches fueron alquilados.

3 La puerta fue abierta.

4 Los ruidos fueron oídos.

5 El trabajo fue terminado.

6 La casa fue construida.

7 Los barcos fueron vendidos.

8 La carta fue leída.

Example:
¿Has visto a mi hermano? Have you seen my brother?
Sí, acabo de verle. Yes, I have just seen him.

1 ¿Ha comprado Vd. los zapatos?

2 ¿Han llegado los invitados?

3 ¿Ha recibido Vd. las cartas?

4 ¿Han hecho Vds. las compras?

5 ¿Se han acostado los niños?

6 ¿Ha encontrado Vd. la llave?

10

CONVERSATION

Marisa y Manolo se encuentran en una cafetería

MANOLO ¡Por fin! Creí que no venías. Llevo aquí más de media hora.

MARISA Lo siento, Manolo. Mi padre necesitaba el coche para ir a ver a unos clientes y he tenido que venir en autobús.

MANOLO Pero el autobús suele ser rápido.

MARISA Generalmente, sí. Pero hoy hemos encontrado una manifestación en la Plaza de San Pedro y el autobús no podía pasar.

MANOLO Y ¿para qué era la manifestación?

MARISA No sé. No he conseguido enterarme. Pero había muchos jóvenes que no dejaban de gritar y que insistían en ponerse delante del autobús.

MANOLO ¡Siempre hay algún jaleo! Bueno ¿qué vas a tomar?

MARISA Tengo sed. Creo que empezaré por tomar una cerveza y después, quizás, algo de comer.

MANOLO Yo acababa de tomar una ginebra con tónica cuando has llegado. Pero voy a tomar otra y un bocadillo de jamón porque tengo hambre.

MARISA ¿Qué vamos a hacer después?

MANOLO Pues había pensado ir al cine ¿que te parece?

MARISA Sí, buena idea. Hay varias películas que me gustaría ver.

MANOLO Ahora decidiremos. Primero voy a llamar al camarero.

10

Marisa and Manolo meet in a Spanish cafeteria

MANOLO   At last! I thought you weren't coming. I've been here more than half an hour.

MARISA   I'm sorry, Manolo. My father needed the car to go and see some clients and I had to come by bus.

MANOLO   But the bus is usually quick.

MARISA   Usually it is. But today we ran into a demonstration in St. Peter's Square and the bus couldn't get through.

MANOLO   And what was the demonstration for?

MARISA   I don't know. I didn't manage to find out. But there were many youngsters who wouldn't stop shouting and who insisted on standing in front of the bus.

MANOLO   There's always some trouble! Well, what are you going to have?

MARISA   I'm thirsty. I think that I'll start by having a beer and then, perhaps, something to eat.

MANOLO   I had just had a gin and tonic when you arrived. But I'm going to have another one and a ham sandwich, because I'm hungry.

MARISA   What are we going to do later?

MANOLO   Well, I thought we could go to the cinema. What do you think?

MARISA   Yes, good idea. There are several films that I would like to see.

MANOLO   We'll decide in a minute (presently). First I'm going to call the waiter.

10

Revision exercises 3

Exercise 1

Put the verbs in italics in the following sentences into the future tense:

1 *Vamos* de paseo después de comer.
2 Pilar *cuida* a los niños.
3 *Trabajo* dos días por semana.
4 *Se levanta* a las ocho.
5 *Salimos* a cenar con unos amigos.
6 *Viene* a vernos el domingo.
7 *Hace* buen tiempo todo el verano.
8 Se lo *dio* al camarero.
9 Este año no *pueden* ir de vacaciones.
10 Ahora *tienes* que hablar espanol.

Exercise 2

This deals with reported speech. Study the examples to see what you have to do, then complete the exercise:

Hablaré al gerente. I'll speak to the manager.
Dijo que hablaría al gerente. He said he would speak to the manager.

Hablaremos al gerente. We'll speak to the manager.
Dijeron que hablarían al gerente. They said they would speak to the manager.

1 Traeré las maletas. Dijo que ….
2 Volveremos a las cinco. Dijeron que ….
3 Viajaré en avión. Dijo que ….
4 Pagaremos por cheque. Dijeron que ….
5 Enviaré una postal. Dijo que ….
6 Tendrán que saberlo pronto. Dijeron que ….

10

Exercise 3

Translate:

1 Last night I saw Antonio with his wife.
2 The train arrived two hours late.
3 He offered to help me with the bags.
4 We didn't need any winter clothes.
5 They sold the house to a friend of theirs.
6 I drove 100 kms. without stopping.
7 He went to look for a chemist's shop.
8 She didn't like the book I gave her.

Exercise 4

Back home after a short holiday in Spain with your wife, you meet a Spanish friend, Alberto, who asks you what you did. Work out what he says, then answer by translating the English lines.

ALBERTO	¿Qué tal lo pasasteis en España?
USTED	Very well. It was a very interesting journey.
ALBERTO	¿Adónde fuisteis?
USTED	We went to Córdoba, Granada and Sevilla.
ALBERTO	¡Qué bien! ¿Habíais estado antes en esas ciudades?
USTED	My wife had been to Sevilla, but I didn't know any of them.
ALBERTO	¿Cuál de ellas te gustó más?
USTED	I don't know. It's difficult to choose one. Each one has a different beauty. Possibly Granada.The Alhambra is wonderful.
ALBERTO	Sí, a mí también me gusta mucho Granada, pero de las tres prefiero Sevilla. Sevilla tiene un encanto especial para mí.
USTED	Alberto, I would like to go on talking, but I have to go shopping with my wife. She'll be waiting for me. I'll call you on Friday.
ALBERTO	Sí, a ver si tomamos una copa juntos. Adiós.

10

Exercise 5

Translate:

1 Why do you need the money?
2 I need it to buy a new car.
3 They left yesterday for Venezuela.
4 I am doing this for you (for your sake).
5 We are too tired to walk to the station.
6 The hotel costs fifty euros per person.
7 He invited me to his house for a month.
8 They sent me a card to tell me they were coming.

Exercise 6

These sentences are all in the passive voice. Rewrite them using one of the means of avoiding the passive given in section 83:

1 Los vuelos han sido cancelados.
2 Fue acompañado por su mujer.
3 La película ha sido censurada.
4 Las elecciones fueron anunciadas en octubre.
5 El muchacho fue arrestado por la policía.
6 La exposición fue inaugurada por el Rey.
7 La explosión fue oída en todo el pueblo.
8 El cheque no ha sido aceptado por el banco.

Exercise 7

Put the correct prepositions after the verbs in the following sentences, if appropriate:

1 Se cansó ... estudiar y salió ... dar un paseo.
2 Mi padre me enseñó ... nadar.
3 Intentamos ... comprar billetes, pero estaba todo vendido.
4 Me ha prometido que va ... dejar ... fumar.
5 La carta tardó ... llegar cinco días.

10

6 Al salir del cine empezó ... llover.

7 Volví ... telefonear, pero no contestaron.

8 Consiguió ... encontrar un empleo en una fábrica.

9 Como no venía el autobús, decidimos ... tomar un taxi.

10 Acabo ... leer una novela buenísima.

11 Insistieron ... devolverme el dinero.

12 Espero ... recibir el paquete mañana.

13 María está aprendiendo ... conducir.

14 Pensamos ... viajar por toda España.

15 Se olvidaron ... darnos su dirección.

16 Siempre sueña ... volver a su país.

Exercise 8

Translate:

1 We are all tired today.

2 My son wants to be a lawyer.

3 When he was ill, I used to visit him every day.

4 Don't sit (fam. sing.) in that chair, it's broken.

5 It's very hot, although all the windows are open.

6 He is sad because his best friend has died.

7 I am always at home on Sundays.

8 She is a very intelligent woman, but not very kind.

9 Who are you (pol. sing.)? I am a friend of hers.

10 We were about to leave when he arrived.

11 They didn't give him the job because he was too young.

12 These are not my suitcases, mine are black.

Exercise 9

Put the verbs in brackets into the correct form of the imperfect tense or the past historic, as appropriate:

1 Siempre que nosotros [ir] a Italia [quedarse] en el mismo hotel.

2 El policía me [hacer] parar el coche y me [pedir] el pasaporte.

3 Les dije que no [tener] dinero y no [poder] pagar la multa.

4 Carmen le [llamar] a la oficina, pero él no [estar].

5 Nosotros [llevar] media hora esperando cuando [llegar] el tren.

6 Ellos [ir] a ver Toledo, pero [volver] pronto porque [hacer] mucho frío.

7 Cuando yo [llegar] al restaurante, mi hermana ya [estar] allí.

8 El portero me [dejar] entrar cuando le [dar] una propina.

9 El avión [salir] con mucho retraso porque [haber] niebla.

10 Pedro [trabajar] durante diez años en una oficina que [estar] cerca de mi casa.

10

Week 11

86 USES OF THE VERB 'DEBER'

The verb **deber** followed by an infinitive translates the English 'must':

Debemos salir temprano.
We must leave early.
No debes fumar tanto.
You mustn't smoke so much.

Used in the conditional, **deber** translates 'should' and 'ought':

Vd. no debería hablar así.
You should not speak like that.
Deberíamos tener más cuidado.
We ought to be more careful.

Deber de followed by an infinitive translates 'must' (expressing assumption):

Deben de tener mucha hambre.
They must be very hungry.
El avión debe de haber llegado ya.
The plane must have arrived already.

Deber also means 'to owe':

Deben mucho dinero. They owe a lot of money.

87 'SABER' AND 'PODER'

It is important not to confuse these two verbs when translating the English 'can'. Compare the following examples:

¿Sabe Vd. conducir?
Can you drive? (= Do you know how to?)
¿Puede Vd. conducir?
Can you drive? (= Are you physically able to?)

VOCABULARY

la cosa	thing
las gafas	glasses
allí	there
a menudo	often
la explicación	explanation
la sortija	ring
costar (ue)	to cost
montar en bicicleta	to ride a bicycle
la píldora	pill
guisar	to cook

11

Translate:

1 How much do I owe you (pol.)?
2 They ought not to say those things.
3 She must have a good job.
4 I must see a doctor.
5 Can he speak Spanish?
6 I cannot read without glasses.
7 We should go there more often.
8 He owes me an explanation.
9 That ring must cost a lot of money.
10 I cannot ride a bicycle.
11 He cannot sleep without taking pills.
12 Can you (pol.) cook?

88 THE PRESENT SUBJUNCTIVE

1 Regular verbs
The present subjunctive of regular verbs is conjugated:

hablar	**comer**	**vivir**
hable	**coma**	**viva**
hables	**comas**	**vivas**
hable	**coma**	**viva**
hablemos	**comamos**	**vivamos**
habléis	**comáis**	**viváis**
habien	**coman**	**vivan**

2 Stem-changing verbs
Stem-changing verbs of the first and second conjugations have the same stem changes as in the present indicative:

cerrar (ie)	**volver (ue)**
cierre	**vuelva**
cierres	**vuelvas**

11

cierre	vuelva
cerremos	volvamos
cerréis	volváis
cierren	vuelvan

Stem-changing verbs of the third conjugation have a stem change also in the first and second persons plural, e changing to i and o changing to u:

pedir (i)	sentir (ie)	dormir (ue)
pida	sienta	duerma
pidas	sientas	duermas
pida	sienta	duerma
pidamos	sintamos	durmamos
pidáis	sintáis	durmáis
pidan	sientan	duerman

3 Other irregular verbs
The stem of the present subjunctive of most irregular verbs is the same as that of the first person singular of the present indicative. For instance:

	Present	Present subjunctive
tener	tengo	tenga, -as, -a, etc
venir	vengo	venga, -as, -a, etc
traer	traigo	traiga, -as, -a, etc
conocer	conozco	conozca, -as, -a, etc

The exceptions to this rule are: **dar, estar, haber, ir, saber,** and **ser**:

dar	estar	haber
dé	esté	haya
des	estés	hayas
dé	esté	haya
demos	estemos	hayamos
deis	estéis	hayáis
den	estén	hayan

11

ir	saber	ser
vaya	sepa	sea
vayas	sepas	seas
vaya	sepa	sea
vayamos	sepamos	seamos
vayáis	sepáis	seáis
vayan	sepan	sean

To differentiate the first and third persons singular of the present subjunctive, the subject pronoun is often used.

89 THE PERFECT SUBJUNCTIVE

The perfect subjunctive is formed with the present of **haber** followed by the appropriate past participle:

… que hayan salido …
… that they may have gone out …
… que hayamos visto …
… that we may have seen …

90 USES OF THE SUBJUNCTIVE

The subjunctive is generally used in dependent clauses in which the action of the verb is presented not as a reality, but as a possibility, something that is yet to happen. It is used:

1 after verbs expressing wish, command, request, need, permission, prohibition, preference, doubt, emotion

For example:
Quieren que cantemos. They want us to sing.
Necesito que me ayudes. I need you to help me.
Prefiero que Vd. lo haga. I prefer you to do it.
Me prohiben que vaya. They forbid me to go.
Siento que esté Vd. enfermo. I am sorry you are ill.

11

Note that when the subject of the dependent verb is the same as that of the main verb, the infinitive construction is used:

Quieren cantar. They want to sing.
Prefiero hacerlo. I prefer to do it.

2 after impersonal expressions which indicate doubt, preference, possibility, probability, necessity

Es preferible que esperemos. It's preferable that we wait.
Es dudoso que vengan. It's doubtful that they will come.
Es posible que lo sepa. It's possible that he knows it.

3 after certain conjunctions when they introduce an uncertain or future action

Se lo daré cuando le vea.
I'll give it to him when I see him.
Tendrán que pagarlo aunque no quieran.
They'll have to pay for it even if they don't want to.

4 after the following related phrases

antes de que	before
hasta que	until
para que	so as to
sin que	without
con tal que	provided that
a no ser que	unless
después de que	after

Lo terminaré antes de que llegue.
I'll finish it before he arrives.
Saldremos sin que nos vean.
We'll go out without their seeing us.

5 after relative pronouns with indefinite negative or interrogative antecedents

11

¿Hay alguien que sepa donde está?
Is there anyone who knows where it is?
No hay un hombre que no quiera triunfar.
There is not a man who doesn't want to succeed.

6 after the following expressions when they introduce a future action

quienquiera, quienesquiera	whoever
cualquiera, cualesquiera	whatever
comoquiera	however
cuandoquiera	whenever
dondequiera	wherever

No quiero verle, quienquiera que sea.
I don't want to see him, whoever he is.
Dondequiera que vaya, siempre llevo mi pasaporte.
Wherever I go, I always carry my passport.

'However' followed by an adjective or an adverb is always rendered in Spanish by **por** + adjective/adverb + the subjunctive tense:

Por mucho que le quieras.
However much you love him.
Por caros que sean.
However expensive they may be.
Por estúpido que parezca.
However stupid it may seem.

VOCABULARY

alegrarse	to be glad
el abogado	lawyer
el documento	document
mandar	to order
dudar	to doubt
sorprender	to surprise
perderse	to lose one's way
la lástima	pity

11

dejar	to let, to allow
el precio	price
tocar	to play (an instrument)
el piano	piano
cuidar de	to look after
el problema	problem
tener éxito	to succeed
la práctica	practice

Exercise 45

Translate:

1 I am glad they are able to come.

2 He wants the lawyer to see the documents.

3 They have ordered us to wait here.

4 I doubt that the sun will come out.

5 It surprises me that she has not written.

6 He has asked me to teach him Spanish.

7 It's possible that they have lost their way.

8 It's a pity that we haven't enough money.

9 It's probable that they will get married.

10 I won't be able to do it unless they help me.

11 We'll go to the cinema, provided you let me pay.

12 He will wait until I return.

13 They will have to eat it, even if they don't like it.

14 There is no-one who can pay that price.

15 Is there anyone who can play the piano?

16 I need a woman to look after the children.

17 We'll find it, wherever it is.

18 He will help you (fam. sing.), whenever you have a problem.

19 However much he may try, he will never succeed.

20 However easy it may seem, one needs practice.

11

THE FAMILIAR IMPERATIVE

The familiar imperative corresponds to the pronouns **tú** and **vosotros**, whereas the polite imperative, as we have already seen, corresponds to **Vd.** and **Vds.**

1 Regular verbs

hablar	habla (tú)	hablad (vosotros)	speak!
comer	come (tú)	comed (vosotros)	eat!
vivir	vive (tú)	vivid (vosotros)	live!

2 Stem-changing verbs: only the singular is irregular

cerrar	cierra (tú)	cerrad (vosotros)	close!
volver	vuelve (tú)	volved (vosotros)	come back!
pedir	pide (tú)	pedid (vosotros)	ask!

3 Irregular verbs: only the singular is irregular

decir	di (tú)	decid (vosotros)	say!
hacer	haz (tú)	haced (vosotros)	do!
ir	ve (tú)	id (vosotros)	go!
oír	oye (tú)	oíd (vosotros)	hear!
poner	pon (tú)	poned (vosotros)	put!
salir	sal (tú)	salid (vosotros)	go out!
ser	sé (tú)	sed (vosotros)	be!
tener	ten (tú)	tened (vosotros)	have!
venir	ven (tú)	venid (vosotros)	come!

The familiar imperative only exists in the positive form; in the negative form the second persons singular and plural of the present subjunctive are used.

No hables (s.).	no habléis (pl.).	Don't speak.
No cierres (s.).	no cerréis (pl.).	Don't close.
No vayas (s.).	no vayáis (pl.).	Don't go.

Object and reflexive pronouns are attached to the end of the verb in the positive form, but they precede the verb in the negative form.

11

Míralo (s.).	**miradlo (pl.).**	Look at it.
No lo mires (s.).	**no lo miréis (pl.).**	Don't look at it.
Siéntate (s.).	**sentaos (pl.).**	Sit down.
No te sientes (s.).	**no os sentéis (pl.).**	Don't sit down.

Note that the final **d** of the plural form is omitted when the reflexive pronoun is attached. The exception is **idos** from the verb **ir**. Note also that in some cases an accent is used to preserve the original stress.

Exercise 46

Put the following verbs into the familiar imperative in both positive and negative forms, singular and plural:

1 Hacerlo.

2 Venir.

3 Acostarse.

4 Aprender.

5 Ponerlo.

6 Escribirla.

7 Gritar.

8 Oírlo.

9 Preocuparse.

10 Dormirse.

VOCABULARY

enfadarse	to get angry
escuchar	to listen
vestirse (i)	to get dressed
callarse	to be quiet
despertar (ie)	to waken
perdonar	to forgive
el error	error
mover (ue)	to move

11

Exercise 47

Translate:

1 Don't get angry. (s.)
2 Listen to me. (pl.)
3 Get dressed. (s.)
4 Don't tell me that. (pl.)
5 Be careful. (pl.)
6 Read it to us. (s.)
7 Be quiet. (pl.)
8 Don't wake me up early. (s.)
9 Forgive my error. (pl.)
10 Don't move the car. (s.)

92 IDIOMATIC USE OF 'SEGUIR'

This verb has two meanings: 'to follow' and, with the present participle of another verb, 'to go on doing something':

El perro siguió a su amo.
The dog followed his master.
Siga Vd. trabajando.
Go on working.

'To go on doing something' can also be rendered by the verb **continuar** followed by the present participle:

La mujer continuó hablando.
The woman went on talking.

93 IDIOMATIC USE OF 'VALER'

This verb can be translated by 'to cost' or 'to be worth':

¿Cuánto vale el billete?
How much does the ticket cost?

Esta pulsera no vale nada.
This bracelet is worthless.
No vale la pena.
It isn't worth it.

Valer has exactly the same irregularities in its
conjugation as **salir**.

Drills 22–23

Example:
¿Tiene mucho dinero? Has he a lot of money?
Sí, debe de tener mucho dinero.
Yes, he must have a lot of money.

1 ¿Está enfermo?

2 ¿Son las cinco?

3 ¿Están muy tristes?

4 ¿Trabaja mucho?

5 ¿Hace muchos años?

6 ¿Están en casa?

Example:
¿Vamos a esperar? Are we going to wait?
Sí, es preferible que esperemos.
Yes, it's better if we wait.

1 ¿Van a comer?

2 ¿Va a irse?

3 ¿Vamos a volver?

4 ¿Van a acostarse?

5 ¿Va a pagar?

6 ¿Vamos a sentarnos?

Drills 24–25

Example:
¿Cierro la puerta? Shall I shut the door?
Sí, ciérrala. Yes, shut it.

1 ¿Pedimos los cafés?
2 ¿Traigo el vino?
3 ¿Llamamos a Miguel?
4 ¿Compro el regalo?
5 ¿Abrimos las ventanas?
6 ¿Ayudo a Pedro?

Example:
¿Han terminado de hablar? Have they finished talking?
No, siguen hablando. No, they are still talking.

1 ¿Han terminado de comer?
2 ¿Ha terminado Juan de leer el periódico?
3 ¿Han terminado Vds. de trabajar?
4 ¿Ha terminado Vd. de pintar?
5 ¿Ha terminado Conchita de cantar?
6 ¿Han terminado de construir la casa?

11

CONVERSATION

La Sra. Ramos habla con su hijo Pablo, de quince años

SRA. RAMOS Pablo, levántate que ya son las diez y media.

PABLO Déjame dormir un poco más. Es sábado y no tengo que ir al colegio.

SRA. RAMOS No, pero necesito que vayas a hacerme unas compras.

PABLO ¿Por qué?

SRA. RAMOS Porque yo no tengo tiempo de salir. Vienen unos invitados a cenar esta noche y tengo mucho que hacer en casa.

PABLO Y ¿adónde tengo que ir?

SRA. RAMOS Quiero que me traigas unas cosas del supermercado, ahora te haré una lista, y que recojas la carne de la carnicería.

PABLO Espero que no me lleve mucho tiempo hacer todo eso.

SRA. RAMOS Pues, cuanto antes te levantes, antes te pondrás en camino.

PABLO ¡Y yo que quería jugar al fútbol con mis amigos esta mañana!

SRA. RAMOS ¡Vamos! Date prisa y tendrás tiempo para todo. Ya te he puesto el desayuno en la mesa.

11

Mrs. Ramos talks with her fifteen-year-old son, Pablo

MRS. RAMOS Pablo, get up. It's half past ten.

PABLO Let me sleep a bit longer. It's Saturday and I don't have to go to school.

MRS. RAMOS No, but I need you to go and do some shopping for me.

PABLO Why?

MRS. RAMOS Because I haven't the time to go out. I have guests coming to dinner this evening and I have a lot to do in the house.

PABLO And where do I have to go?

MRS. RAMOS I want you to bring me a few things from the supermarket – I'll make you a list presently – and to pick up the meat from the butcher's.

PABLO I hope it doesn't take me long to do all that.

MRS. RAMOS Well, the sooner you get up the sooner you'll be on your way.

PABLO And I wanted to play football with my friends this morning!

MRS. RAMOS Come on! Hurry up and you'll have time for everything. I've already put your breakfast on the table.

11

Week 12

- formation and use of the imperfect and pluperfect subjunctive
- use of the subjunctive in 'if' clauses and main clauses
- 'may' and 'might'
- verbs followed by prepositions
- 'al' followed by the infinitive

94 THE IMPERFECT SUBJUNCTIVE

The imperfect subjunctive has two forms, with different endings. The stem is obtained by removing the ending **-ron** from the third person plural of the past historic: **habla-, comie-, vivie-**, etc. To this stem the following endings are added either **-ra, -ras, -ra, -ramos, -rais, -ran** or **-se, -ses, -se, semos, -seis, -sen**. Both forms are equally acceptable. It is very much a matter a choice whether one or the other is used.

1 Regular verbs

hablar	hablara, hablaras, etc
	hablase, hablases, etc
comer	comiera, comieras, etc
	comiese, comieses, etc
vivir	viviera, vivieras, etc
	viviese, vivieses, etc

2 Stem-changing verbs

cerrar	cerrara, cerraras, etc
	cerrase, cerrases, etc
volver	volviera, volvieras, etc
	volviese, volvieses, etc
pedir	pidiera, pidieras, etc
	pidiese, pidieses, etc

3 Irregular verbs

| estar | estuviera, estuvieras, etc |
| | estuviese, estuvieses, etc |

12

tener	**tuviera, tuvieras, etc**
	tuviese, tuvieses, etc
decir	**dijera, dijeras, etc**
	dijese, dijeses, etc

95 PLUPERFECT SUBJUNCTIVE

This tense is formed with the imperfect subjunctive of **haber** followed by the past participle of the verb:

Hubiera (hubiese) visto.
He might have seen.
Hubiéramos (hubiésemos) vendido.
We might have sold.

96 USES OF THE IMPERFECT AND PLUPERFECT SUBJUNCTIVE

These tenses are used under the same conditions as the present and perfect subjunctive, but they generally follow a different tense in the main clause. Compare the following examples:

Quiere que lo compres.
He wants you to buy it.
Quería que lo compraras.
He wanted you to buy it.
Espero que haya llegado.
I hope he has arrived.
Esperaba que hubiera llegado.
I hoped he had arrived.
Me dice que le escriba.
He tells me to write to him.
Me dijo que le escribiera.
He told me to write to him.
Es importante que lo haga.
It's important that he does it.
Era importante que lo hiciese.
It was important that he did it.

12

The present and perfect subjunctive usually follow the present indicative, the future, the imperative, and the perfect.

The imperfect and pluperfect subjunctive usually follow the imperfect indicative, the past historic, the conditional, and the pluperfect.

Occasionally the imperfect and pluperfect subjunctive may follow a verb in the present indicative:

Siento mucho que no pudiera venir.
I'm very sorry he could not come.
No es posible que lo supieran.
It's not possible that they knew.
No creo que nos hubieran invitado.
I don't think they would have invited us.

VOCABULARY

viajar	to travel
el accidente	accident
poner la mesa	to lay the table
darse prisa	to hurry
esperar	to hope
avisar	to warn
usar	to use
la máquina	machine
reservar	to book
la persona	person
traducir	to translate
ganar	to win
el premio	prize

12

Exercise 48

Translate:

1 They wanted me to travel with them.

2 I was afraid that he might have had an accident.

3 She told us to lay the table.

4 I asked him to hurry up.

5 We hoped that it would not be too hot in Seville.

6 Wherever he went, he always found friends.

7 I warned him not to use that machine.

8 He phoned me so that I would book the rooms.

9 They were looking for a person who could translate the letter.

10 I am glad that they won the first prize.

98 USE OF THE SUBJUNCTIVE IN 'IF' CLAUSES

The subjunctive is used in an 'if' clause when the action of the verb is uncertain or hypothetical:

Lo compraría si tuviese el dinero.
I would buy it if I had the money.
Acabaríamos antes si me ayudaras.
We would finish sooner if you helped me.

When the action of the verb can be fulfilled, the indicative is used:

Lo compraré si tengo el dinero.
I'll buy it if I have the money.
Acabaremos antes si me ayudas.
We'll finish sooner if you help me.

When the main verb is a conditional perfect, it is usually replaced by the **-ra** form of the pluperfect subjunctive:

No le hubiera insultado si no me hubiese provocado.
I would not have insulted him if he had not provoked me.

The future and conditional tenses are not used with **si** except when it means 'whether':

No sé si vendrá. I don't know whether he will come.
No me dijo si lo vendería.
He didn't tell me whether he would sell it.

VOCABULARY

el perro	dog	**quedarse**	to stay
morder (ue)	to bite	**más tiempo**	longer
pegar	to hit	**el paraguas**	umbrella
guardar	to keep	**mojarse**	to get
el bolsillo	pocket		wet
divertirse (ie)	to have a good time	**el concierto**	concert

Exercise 49

Translate:

1 I would do it, if I could.
2 If the weather is fine, I'll work in the garden.
3 The dog would not have bitten you, if you had not hit it.
4 If you asked them, they wouldn't know what to say.
5 If I saw him now, I would not speak to him.
6 You (polite) would not have lost the money, if you had kept it in your pocket.
7 If they came to the party, they would have a good time.
8 I shall write to you, if I have to stay there longer.
9 If you don't take an umbrella, you'll get wet.
10 I would go to the concert, if he'd come with me.

12

The subjunctive is used:

1 in all imperatives, except the positive familiar imperative

Hable Vd., hablen Vds.
Speak (polite).
No hable Vd., no hablen Vds., no hables, no habléis.
Don't speak (polite and familiar).
but
Habla, hablad. Speak (familiar).

2 to express a wish

¡Que tenga Vd. buen viaje! Have a good journey!
¡Que se mejore Vd.! Get well soon!
¡Que sean muy felices! May they be very happy!

3 after the word **ojalá** ('if only', 'would that ...')

¡Ojalá pudiera verle!
If only I could see him!
¡Ojalá ganáramos la lotería!
Would that we won the lottery!

4 after **quizá(s), tal vez, acaso** ('perhaps'). Sometimes the indicative is used, depending on the degree of doubt

Quizá no venga hoy.
Perhaps he won't come today.
Acaso no lo sepan.
Perhaps they don't know it.
Tal vez no habían oído la noticia.
Perhaps they hadn't heard the news.

5 in certain set expressions

Sea como sea. Be that as it may.
Sea lo que sea. Whatever it is.
Pase lo que pase. Whatever happens.

12

Diga lo que diga. Whatever he says.
Hagan lo que hagan. Whatever they do.

6 to translate the English 'let'

Que espere. Let him wait.
Que paguen. Let them pay.

100 'MAY' AND 'MIGHT'

When they indicate possibility, 'may' and 'might' can be translated by any of the following expressions:

puede que, es posible que, quizá(s), tal vez: may
pudiera, era posible que, quizá(s), tal vez: might

Puede que estén trabajando. They may be working.
Es posible que llueva. It may rain.
Pensó que pudiera haber ocurrido.
He thought that it might have happened.
Dijo que era posible que volvieran.
He said that they might return.

When 'may' and 'might' are used to express permission, they are translated by the present or imperfect indicative:

¿Puedo entrar? May I come in?
Dijeron que podíamos jugar con ellos.
They said we might play with them.

VOCABULARY

perder	to miss (a train, boat, etc)
estar en contacto con	to be in touch with
la fotografía	photograph
el día libre	day off
el aviso	warning (sign)

12

Exercise 50

Translate:

1 If only I did not have to work.
2 Perhaps he is ill.
3 We may have missed the train.
4 Let him come, if he likes.
5 If only we could have a holiday.
6 Whatever happens, I'll be in touch with you (pol.).
7 May we see the photographs?
8 He said that I might have the day off.
9 Have a good time! (pol.)
10 Perhaps they did not see the warning sign.

101 VERBS FOLLOWED BY PREPOSITIONS

In section 85 we have seen some common verbs that have a preposition before an infinitive. Here now are some verbs that have a preposition before the object of the verb.

acercarse a (to approach, to go near)
El hombre se acercó a la casa.
The man approached the house.

asomarse a (to lean out of)
La niña se asomó a la ventana.
The girl leaned out of the window.

casarse con (to marry)
Por fin se casó con ella.
In the end he did marry her.

contar con (to count on, to rely on)
No puedo contar con mi hermano.
I cannot rely on my brother.

dar a (to overlook)
Los balcones daban al mar.
The balconies overlooked the sea.

12

depender de (to depend on)
El resultado no depende de mí.
The result does not depend on me.

despedirse de (to say goodbye to)
Vinieron a despedirse de nosotros.
They came to say goodbye to us.

dudar de (to doubt)
No dude Vd. de su palabra.
Do not doubt his word.

enamorarse de (to fall in love with)
Se enamoró de una chica muy joven.
He fell in love with a very young girl.

encontrarse con (to meet, to come across)
Me encontré con un viejo amigo.
I came across an old friend.

enterarse de (to find out, to hear about)
No me había enterado de su muerte.
I had not heard about his death.

fijarse en (to notice)
¿Se ha fijado Vd. en el sombrero de Anita?
Have you noticed Anita's hat?

ocuparse de (to attend to)
Nos ocuparemos de los invitados.
We'll attend to the guests.

parecerse a (to resemble, to look like)
No se parece a su padre.
He doesn't look like his father.

pensar en (to think of)
Siempre está pensando en sus hijos.
He is always thinking of his children.

12

pensar de (to think of, to have an opinion on)
¿Qué piensa Vd. de esa película?
What do you think of that film?

saber a (to taste of)
Este pastel sabe a canela.
This cake tastes of cinnamon.

soñar con (to dream of)
Anoche soñé contigo.
Last night I dreamt of you.

VOCABULARY

el borde	edge
la ventanilla	window (of a vehicle)
concurrido (-a)	busy, crowded
el éxito	success
la obra (de teatro)	play
el compañero	colleague, companion
la buena intención	goodwill
tonto (-a)	silly
fácil	easy
el/la turista	tourist
el nombre	name
la situación	situation
el helado	ice cream
la fresa	strawberry
el lugar	place

12

Exercise 51

Translate:

1 Don't go near the edge.
2 He leaned out of the car window.
3 My brother is going to marry an English girl.
4 You know that you can count on me.
5 The window overlooked a very busy street.
6 The success of the play depends on the actors.
7 I have to say goodbye to my colleagues.
8 They don't doubt his goodwill.
9 Maria has fallen in love with a very silly man.
10 It's very easy to meet American tourists in Spain.
11 We have not been able to find out his name.
12 I didn't notice what she was wearing.
13 You have to attend to the drinks.
14 This house looks very much like ours.
15 He doesn't want to think of all the problems.
16 We don't know what he thinks of the situation.
17 This ice cream tastes of strawberry.
18 I was dreaming of all the places I had visited.

102 'AL' FOLLOWED BY INFINITIVE

This translates the English 'on' + present participle:

Le vi al salir del hotel.
I saw him on leaving the hotel.
Al entrar en el cuarto todo el mundo dejó de hablar.
On entering the room everybody stopped talking.

It may also translate sentences with 'when' and 'as':

Sonrió al verme.
He smiled when he saw me.
Le saludé con la mano al entrar.
I waved at him as I came in.

12

Drills 26–27

Example:
¿Va a venir? Is he going to come?
Puede que venga. He may come.

1 ¿Va Vd. a venderlo?

2 ¿Van a casarse?

3 ¿Van Vds. a salir?

4 ¿Va a volver?

5 ¿Van a invitarnos?

6 ¿Va Vd. a nadar?

Change the verb in the future into the conditional,
followed by the appropriate form of the subjunctive.
Thus:
Lo compraré si tengo dinero.
I'll buy it if I have the money.

Lo compraría si tuviera dinero.
I'd buy it if I had the money.

1 Vendrán si pueden.

2 Lo pediremos si lo necesitamos.

3 Comeré si tengo hambre.

4 Se lo diremos si le vemos.

5 Saldrán si no llueve.

6 Te lo daré si lo encuentro.

7 Trabajará más si le pagan bien.

8 Hablaré con ellos si vienen.

12

Drill 28

Example:
Se pararon cuando llegaron al puente.
They stopped when they arrived at the bridge.
Se pararon al llegar al puente.
They stopped on arriving at the bridge.

1 Se sorprendió cuando oyó la noticia.
2 Gritaron cuando vieron a los policías.
3 Lloraba cuando leía la carta.
4 Me pidió la llave cuando salía.
5 Tuve miedo cuando oí un ruido.
6 Se lavaron las manos cuando terminaron.
7 Me quité el sombrero cuando entré.
8 Empezó a llover cuando llegamos a casa.

12

Una invitación a cenar

[El teléfono suena.]

ALFONSO **¡Dígame!**

PILAR **¿Eres Alfonso?**

ALFONSO **Sí. ¿Quién es?**

PILAR **Soy Pilar.**

ALFONSO **¡Hola Pilar! No te había conocido. ¿Cómo estás?**

PILAR **Muy bien. ¿Y tú?**

ALFONSO **Bien, gracias. ¿Querías hablar con Conchita? Ha ido a recoger a los niños al colegio.**

PILAR **¡Ah! Bueno, no importa. La razón por la que llamo es para ver si tú y Conchita queréis venir a cenar el viernes.**

ALFONSO **El viernes no podemos porque llega mi madre de Barcelona a pasar unos días con nosotros, y tenemos que ir al aeropuerto a las nueve de la noche. Lo siento mucho, Pilar.**

PILAR **No te preocupes. ¿Podéis venir el sábado?**

ALFONSO **El sábado, sí. Lo único es que no me gustaría dejar sola a mi madre.**

PILAR **Pues, que venga también. Encantada de tener una invitada más.**

ALFONSO **En ese caso, estupendo. ¿A qué hora nos esperas?**

PILAR **¿Te parece bien a las ocho? Así tenemos tiempo de tomar un aperitivo antes de cenar.**

ALFONSO **Muy bien. Se lo diré a Conchita. Hasta el sábado y gracias.**

PILAR **De nada. Adiós.**

12

An invitation to dinner

[The phone rings.]

ALFONSO Hello!

PILAR Is that Alfonso?

ALFONSO Yes. Who is it?

PILAR It's Pilar.

ALFONSO Hello Pilar! I didn't recognize your voice. How are you?

PILAR Very well. And you?

ALFONSO Fine, thanks. Did you want to speak to Conchita? She has gone to collect the children from school.

PILAR Oh! Well, it doesn't matter. The reason I'm ringing is to see if you and Conchita would like to come to dinner on Friday.

ALFONSO We can't on Friday, because my mother is coming from Barcelona to spend a few days with us, and we have to go to the airport at nine o'clock in the evening. I'm sorry, Pilar.

PILAR Don't worry. Can you come on Saturday?

ALFONSO On Saturday, yes. The only thing is I would not like to leave my mother alone.

PILAR Well, let her come too. Delighted to have one more guest.

ALFONSO In that case, fine. What time do you expect us?

PILAR Is eight o'clock all right for you? That way we'll have time to have a drink before dinner.

ALFONSO Very well. I'll tell Conchita. Till Saturday and thank you.

PILAR Not at all. 'Bye.

12

Week 13

- how to use some important verbs in different contexts
- 'más' and 'menos'
- 'tan' and 'tal'
- 'pero' and 'sino'
- some more prepositions
- augmentatives and diminutives
- idiomatic uses of certain verbs

103 SOME IMPORTANT VERBS

It is important that you should learn not only the meaning of the following verbs, but also how to use them in a variety of different contexts.

asistir (to assist, to attend)
Tuve que asistir al herido.
I had to assist the injured man.
Asistimos a una representación de Aída.
We attended a performance of Aida.

bastar (to be enough, to suffice)
No basta decírselo.
It's not enough to tell him.
Este pan nos basta para el desayuno.
This bread is enough for our breakfast.

caber (to fit in)
No cabemos todos en un coche.
We don't all fit into one car.
Este armario no cabe en esa habitación.
This wardrobe does not fit into that room.

devolver (to return, to give back)
Me ha devuelto mi carta. He has returned my letter.
Nos devolvieron el dinero. They refunded our money.

echar (to throw, to pour)
Eché la carta al fuego. I threw the letter on the fire.
Echó el té en la taza. She poured the tea in the cup.

faltar (to lack, to be missing)
No le falta inteligencia.
He doesn't lack intelligence.
Faltan dos páginas en este libro.
There are two pages missing in this book.

hacer falta (to need)
No hace falta ir más lejos. There's no need to go further.
Me hace falta más gasolina. I need more petrol.

meter (to put in, to insert)
Metió la llave en la cerradura.
He put the key in the lock.
Me metí la mano en el bolsillo.
I put my hand in my pocket.

quedar (to remain, to have left)
Quedan cuatro lecciones. There remain four lessons.
Me quedan cuarenta dólares. I have forty dollars left.

quitar(se) (to take away, to take off)
Le quitaron el pasaporte. They took his passport.
Me quité los zapatos. I took off my shoes.

sobrar (to have more than enough, to have to spare)
Sobran candidatos para ese trabajo.
There are more than enough candidates for that job.
¿Te sobra algo de dinero?
Have you any money to spare?

tocar (to touch, to play an instrument)
No toque Vd. la pintura.
Don't touch the paint.
Toca la guitarra maravillosamente.
He plays the guitar beautifully.

tomar (to take, to have food or drink)
Tomó al niño en sus brazos.
He took the child in his arms.
Vamos a tomar un café.
Let's have a coffee.

13

la gente	people	el ayudante	helper
el entierro	funeral	la silla	chair
la cantidad	amount	la chaqueta	jacket
la harina	flour	el huevo	egg
la caja	box	la tortilla	omelet
el maletero	car boot	la seda	silk
prestar	to lend	el violín	violin
la pelota	ball	firmar	to sign
el estante	shelf		

Exercise 52

Translate:

1 Many people attended the funeral.

2 This amount of flour will be enough.

3 That box doesn't fit in the boot of the car.

4 I want to return the magazine he lent me.

5 He threw the ball to the children.

6 I am going to pour the wine.

7 They lack experience.

8 There are five books missing from this shelf.

9 We need more helpers.

10 They will put all the clothes in one suitcase.

11 How many days have you left?

12 He will take away these chairs.

13 May I take off my jacket?

14 There are more than enough eggs to make the omelet.

15 It's very pleasant to touch silk.

16 He would like to play the violin.

17 He took the pen and signed the letter.

18 They like to have wine with their meal.

13

104 'MÁS' AND 'MENOS'

We have already seen these two words in the comparatives **más que** (more than) and **menos que** (less than). But when 'more than' and 'less than' are followed by a numeral, they are translated by **más de** and **menos de**.

For example:
Hay más de quinientos alumnos en esa escuela.
There are more than five hundred pupils in that school.
He pagado menos de tres euros.
I have paid less than three euros.

In the negative, **que** replaces **de** and **no ... más que** is translated by 'only':

No tengo más que un hermano.
I have only one brother.
No hay más que tres manzanas.
There are only three apples.

When **más de** and **menos** de are followed by a clause, the forms **el que, la que, los que, las que** must be used. If no definite noun is referred to, **lo que** is used.

For example:
Tenemos más comida de la que necesitamos.
We have more food than we need.
Es más inteligente de lo que parece.
He is more intelligent than he looks.

105 'TAN' AND 'TAL'

Both words translate the English 'such', but **tan** precedes an adjective whereas **tal(es)** precedes a noun.

Es un libro tan interesante. It's such an interesting book.
No conozco a tal hombre. I don't know such a man.

13

Tan is also used in exclamations:

¡Qué casa tan bonita!
What a lovely house!
¡Qué día tan horrible!
What a horrible day!

The adjective **semejante** can also translate 'such':

No diga Vd. semejante cosa.
Don't say such a thing.

106 'PERO' AND 'SINO'

Although 'but' is generally translated by **pero**, remember to use **sino** after a negative statement when 'but' introduces a clause that is contrary to the first statement:

Este regalo no es para mi madre, sino para mi hermana.
This present is not for my mother, but for my sister.
No he pedido carne, sino pescado.
I haven't ordered meat, but fish.

VOCABULARY

heredar	to inherit
el collar	necklace
feo	ugly
el edificio	building
aburrido	boring
listo	clever

13

Exercise 53

Translate:

1 He has inherited more than a million euros.

2 I cannot sell it for less than a hundred euros.

3 We have lived in Madrid more than fifteen years.

4 I shall do it in less than five minutes.

5 He had never seen such a beautiful necklace.

6 What an ugly building!

7 He wouldn't do such a thing

8 I find such books very boring.

9 That is not my brother, but my cousin.

10 They don't have a dog, but they have two cats.

11 He has more money than he says.

12 They are cleverer than you think.

13 What a good idea!

14 It is such a long journey!

107 PREPOSITIONS

Here is a list of the most common simple and compound prepositions. **Por** and **para** are not included, as they have been dealt with in section 81.

a (to, at)
Used for 'at' in expressions of time and a few set phrases such as **a la mesa** 'at table' and **a la puerta** 'at the door'.

Van a la playa.
They go to the beach.
Te veré a las ocho.
I'll see you at eight.
Nos sentamos a la mesa.
We sat at the table.

ante (before)
When meaning 'in the presence of', 'faced with'.

13

Ante ese problema, no supo que hacer.
Faced with that problem, he didn't know what to do.
Se presentó ante el tribunal.
He appeared before the court.

antes de (before time)
Llegaremos antes de las cuatro.
We shall arrive before four o'clock.

bajo (under)
Trabaja bajo su dirección.
He works under him.

debajo de (under = underneath)
Encontré la sortija debajo del sillón.
I found the ring under the armchair.

con (with)
Iremos con Juan. We'll go with John.
¿Quiere Vd. venir conmigo?
Do you want to come with me?

contra (against)
Ponga Vd. esa silla contra la pared.
Put that chair against the wall.

de (of, from, about)
La casa de Conchita.
Conchita's house.
Estamos hablando de Vd.
We are talking about you.
Trabajo de nueve a dos.
I work from nine till two.

delante de (in front of)
Andaba delante de mí.
He was walking in front of me.

desde (from, more emphatic than **de**)
Desde la ventana se ve el mar.
From the window one can see the sea.

13

después de (after = time)
Después de cenar daremos un paseo.
After dinner we shall go for a walk.

detrás de (behind)
El garaje está detrás de la casa.
The garage is behind the house.

en (in, on, at)
El regalo está en la caja.
The present is in the box.
La comida está en la mesa.
The food is on the table.
Estarán en casa todo el día.
They will be at home all day.

encima de (on top of, over)
La maleta está encima del armario.
The suitcase is on top of the wardrobe.

enfrente de (opposite)
La farmacia está enfrente del banco.
The chemist's is opposite the bank.

entre (between)
Podemos pagar los gastos entre nosotros.
We can pay the expenses between us.

hacia (towards, about = of time)
El niño vino hacia nosotros.
The boy came towards us.
Volveremos hacia el veinte de septiembre.
We shall come back towards the 20th of September.

hasta (until, as far as)
Durmió hasta las once.
He slept until eleven.
Me acompañó hasta la parada de autobús.
He accompanied me as far as the bus stop.

13

según (according to)
Según el hombre del tiempo, va a llover.
According to the weather man, it's going to rain.

sin (without)
No podemos viajar sin pasaporte.
We cannot travel without a passport.

sobre (on, upon, about)
Las cartas están sobre la mesa.
The letters are on the table.
Tenemos que hablar sobre ese tema.
We have to talk about that subject.

tras (after)
El perro corrió tras la pelota.
The dog ran after the ball.

VOCABULARY

espléndido	generous
la fila	line, row
el juez	judge
la cama	bed
la zapatería	shoe shop
la panadería	bakery
el piso	floor
probar	to try, to test
el sofá	sofa
el paquete	parcel
el escritorio	desk

13

Exercise 54

Translate:

1 The man was sleeping under a tree.
2 He wrote to me from Córdoba.
3 After the theatre, we went to his house.
4 He is very generous with his friends.
5 We waited at the door, but he did not come.
6 According to his father, he is very ill.
7 There was a long line of cars in front of me.
8 He had to appear before the judge.
9 They left without paying for the drink.
10 He put the suitcase under the bed.
11 There is a shoe shop opposite the bakery.
12 I won't see you until Sunday.
13 The lift stopped between the two floors.
14 I want to try it before buying it.
15 We shall start walking towards the station.
16 They will have to go on the bus.
17 The book has fallen behind the sofa.
18 I shall leave the parcel on top of the desk.

108 AUGMENTATIVES AND DIMINUTIVES

Certain augmentative and diminutive endings are added to nouns, to qualify their meaning. As the use of these terminations can present considerable difficulties, without a thorough knowledge of the language, the student is advised to employ adjectives instead.

1 Augmentatives

-ón, **-azo**, **-acho**, **-ote** express largeness and may also imply some degree of awkwardness or ugliness:

un hombrón a big man
unos ojazos big eyes
una mujerona a big woman

13

2 Diminutives

-ito, **-ico**, **-illo**, **-uelo** express smallness and sometimes fondness on the part of the speaker:

un perrito a little dog
un corrillo a small circle of people
un polluelo a chick

Many augmentatives and diminutives have established themselves as words in their own right:

ventana (window)→ **ventanilla** (window of a vehicle)
silla (chair)→ **sillín** (saddle)**, sillón** (armchair)
puerta (door)→ **portezuela** (door of a vehicle)
cera (wax)→ **cerillas** (matches)
caja (box)→ **cajón** (drawer)
camisa (shirt)→ **camisón** (night dress)
pan (bread)→ **panecillo** (roll)
niebla (fog)→ **neblina** (mist)

109 IDIOMATIC USES OF CERTAIN VERBS

The following lists give examples of idiomatic uses and meanings of some important verbs.

1 caer (to fall)

La pobre mujer cayó enferma y murió a las dos semanas.
The poor woman fell ill and died two weeks later.

Es un hombre que me cae mal.
He is a man I dislike.

Ese vestido te cae muy bien.
That dress fits you very well.

No han caído en la cuenta.
They haven't 'caught on'.

2 dar (to give)

Vamos a dar un paseo / Vamos a dar una vuelta.
Let's go for a walk.
Las dos hermanas se dieron un abrazo.
The two sisters embraced each other.

Al ver al ladrón, di un grito.
On seeing the burglar, I screamed.

Las ventanas de los dormitorios dan a una pequeña plaza.
The bedroom windows overlook a little square.

No olvides dar de comer al perro.
Don't forget to feed the dog.

No se dio cuenta del error.
He didn't realize the mistake.

No puedo seguir jugando, me doy por vencido.
I can't go on playing, I give up.

Es tarde, tenemos que dar la vuelta.
It's late, we have to turn back.

Voy a darle los buenos días a tu madre.
I am going to say good morning to your mother.

Tenemos que darnos prisa o no llegaremos a tiempo.
We have to hurry or we won't be on time.

Han ido a dar parte del robo a la policía.
They have gone to report the theft to the police.

Al despedirse, se dieron la mano.
As they said goodbye, they shook hands.

Podemos tomar vino blanco o tinto, lo mismo me da.
We can have white or red wine, it's all the same to me.

13

3 dejar(se) (to allow, to leave behind)

Sus padres no le dejan salir.
His parents won't let him go out.
Hemos dejado el coche en el aparcamiento.
We have left the car in the car park.

Me dejé el paraguas en el taxi.
I left my umbrella in the taxi.

4 dejar de (to give up, to stop)

¿Cuándo vas a dejar de trabajar?
When are you going to stop working?

No dejes de llamarme.
Do call me.

5 despedir(se) (to dismiss, to say goodbye to)

Han despedido a cien empleados.
They have dismissed one hundred employees.

Carmen vino a despedirme al aeropuerto.
Carmen came to see me off at the airport.

6 echar (to throw)

Echa estos periódicos a la basura.
Throw these newspapers in the bin.

Tenemos que echar estas cartas antes de las cuatro.
We have to post these letters before four o'clock.

No debes echar la culpa a Juan.
You mustn't blame Juan.

Cuando vi el autobús, eché a correr, pero no pude cogerlo.
When I saw the bus, I started to run, but I couldn't catch it.

13

Me gusta vivir en Nueva York, pero echo de menos el clima del Mediterráneo.
I like living in New York, but I miss the Mediterranean climate.

Siempre está dispuesto a echar una mano.
He is always ready to lend a hand.

No olvides echar la llave a la puerta.
Don't forget to lock the door.

7 llevar(se) (to carry, to take, to wear)

Tuvimos que llevarle al médico.
We had to take him to the doctor.

No me gusta llevar sombrero.
I don't like to wear a hat.

Los dos hermanos se llevan muy bien.
The two brothers get on very well.

Mi marido me lleva cuatro años.
My husband is four years older than I.

No le gusta cuando le llevan la contraria.
He doesn't like it when they contradict him.

Viven en el campo y llevan una vida muy tranquila.
They live in the country and they lead a very quiet life.

8 valer (to be worth, to cost)

¿Cuánto vale el alquiler del coche?
How much is the car hire?

Más vale ir directamente al hotel.
It's better to go straight to the hotel.

No vale la pena esperar.
It's not worth waiting.

13

Drills 29–31

Example:
¿Necesita Vd. el paraguas ? Do you need the umbrella?
No, no me hace falta. No, I don't need it.
¿Necesitan Vds. sellos? Do you need stamps?
No, no nos hacen falta. No, we don't need them.

1 ¿Necesita Carmen el coche?

2 ¿Necesitan Vds. el pasaporte?

3 ¿Necesita Vd. estas cajas?

4 ¿Necesitan ellos ayuda?

5 ¿Necesita Ramón las gafas?

6 ¿Necesitan Vds. otra maleta?

Example:
Ha firmado Vd. la carta? Have you signed the letter?
No puedo firmarla todavía. I cannot sign it yet.

1 ¿Han devuelto Vds. el dinero?

2 ¿Ha metido Vd. la ropa en la maleta?

3 ¿Han echado ellos las postales?

4 ¿Se ha quitado Vd. los zapatos?

5 ¿Han tomado Vds. vino?

6 ¿Ha pagado Carlos la cuenta?

Fill in the blanks with the appropriate preposition from the column on the right.

1	Trabajaré … las cinco.	en
2	Nos escribirá … Sevilla.	sin
3	El hotel está … la playa.	hacia
4	He dejado la maleta … la cama.	antes de
5	… los dos podemos mover el armario.	enfrente de
6	No puedes salir … abrigo.	desde
7	Queremos habla … el gerente.	encima de
8	No podré llegar … las diez.	con
9	Te esperaremos … casa.	entre
10	Los niños corrieron … su padre.	hasta

13

En el tren

FELIPE ¿Perdone, está ocupado este asiento?

LOLITA No, no creo.

FELIPE Menos mal. Creí que no iba a encontrar sitio. El tren está casi lleno.

LOLITA Es verdad. Nunca he visto tanta gente en este tren.

FELIPE ¿Le importa que cierre la cortina? Entre demasiado sol.

LOLITA No, ciérrela, si quiere. A mi también mi molesta.

FELIPE ¿Quiere Vd. un chicle?

LOLITA De qué sabor son?

FELIPE Son de fresa.

LOLITA Si, gracias. Me encantan los chicles de fresa .... Bueno, parece que nos ponemos en marcha. ¿Va Vd. a Segovia?

FELIPE Sí. Tengo que visitar una fábrica allí. No voy a estar más que dos días. ¿Y Vd.?

LOLITA Yo también voy a Segovia, a pasar una semana con unos amigos. ¡Ay, qué rabia! He olvidado comprar algo para leer en el viaje.

FELIPE ¿Quiere Vd. esta revista?

LOLITA Si a Vd. no le hace falta de momento, me gustaría verla. Gracias.

13

On the train

FELIPE Excuse me. Is this seat taken?

LOLITA No, I don't think so.

FELIPE Thank goodness. I thought I wasn't going to find a place. The train is almost full.

LOLITA It's true. I have never seen so many people on this train.

FELIPE Do you mind if I close the blind? There's too much sun coming in.

LOLITA No, close it if you want. I don't like too much sun either.

FELIPE Would you like a chewing gum?

LOLITA Which flavour are they?

FELIPE They're strawberry flavour.

LOLITA Yes, thanks. I love strawberry chewing gum .... Well, it looks as if we're moving. Are you going to Segovia?

FELIPE Yes. I have to visit a factory there. I'm only going to stay a couple of days. And you?

LOLITA I'm going to Segovia too, to spend a week with some friends. Oh, bother! I've forgotten to buy something to read on the journey.

FELIPE Would you like this magazine?

LOLITA If you don't need it for the moment, I'd like to look at it. Thanks.

13

Revision exercises 4

Exercise 1

Translate:

1 They must have gone out.
2 She could neither read nor write.
3 We ought to wait a few more minutes.
4 Can you (pol. sing.) tell me the time?
5 He was afraid because he could not swim.
6 You (fam. sing.) should invite her to dinner.
7 They owe me twelve euros.
8 You (fam. pl.) must decide what you want to do.

Exercise 2

Put the verbs in brackets into the correct form of the present subjunctive:

1 Quiere que nosotros [ir] con él.
2 Necesito que ella me [ayudar] en la cocina.
3 Es preferible que ellos [quedarse] en casa.
4 Le han prohibido que [salir].
5 No quieren que yo lo [saber].
6 Sentimos que usted no [poder] venir.
7 Es probable que [llover] hoy.
8 Me alegro de que vosotros [tener] éxito.
9 No le gusta que su hija [jugar] con esos niños.
10 No quiero que tú [llegar] tarde.
11 Se lo diremos cuando le [ver].
12 Esperaremos hasta que él [venir].
13 Dígale a Paco que me [llamar].
14 Dudo que ellos [tener] suficiente dinero.
15 No debes permitirle que lo [hacer].
16 ¿Hay alguien que me [acompañar]?

13

Exercise 3

Use the verbs in brackets in the following phrases to make commands using the 'tú' form:

1 [Esperar] un momento.
2 [Sentarse] aquí.
3 [Darle] las llaves.
4 [Hacer] el café.
5 No [pedir] más caramelos.
6 [Tener] cuidado.
7 No [traer] al perro.
8 [Venir] pasado mañana.

Exercise 4

Use the verbs in brackets in the following phrases to make commands using the 'vosotros' form:

1 [Limpiar] vuestra habitación.
2 No [volver] a casa tarde.
3 [Comer] en la cafetería.
4 [Acostarse] temprano.
5 No [decirle] que estoy enfermo.
6 No [ir] a España en agosto.
7 [Escribir] vuestro nombre aquí.
8 No [telefonearme] antes de las once.

13

Exercise 5

Put the verbs in brackets into either of the correct forms of the subjunctive:

1 Nos extrañó que él no [estar] allí.
2 Le dije que me lo [enviar] al hotel.
3 Nos pidió que le [perdonar].
4 No quisieron que yo [ir] al aeropuerto.
5 Te lo diríamos si lo [saber].
6 Ojalá tú [poder] venir de vacaciones conmigo.
7 Era importante que ellos [firmar] ese documento.
8 Podrían comer en el jardín si [hacer] mejor tiempo.
9 Yo no estaría aquí si eso [ser] verdad.
10 Pedro no te daría dinero aunque tú lo [necesitar].
11 Nos aconsejó que no [vender] la casa.
12 Me dijo que [traer] el pasaporte.

Exercise 6

Your friend Paco, whom you haven't seen for some time, rings you to arrange a meeting. Answer him in Spanish.

PACO Te llamo porque hace mucho tiempo que no nos vemos.
USTED I know. I've had a lot of work.
PACO ¿Por qué no vamos a cenar mañana?
USTED I am sorry. I haven't any free evenings this week.
PACO Entonces, díme cuándo podemos vernos.
USTED Saturday of next week?
PACO ¡Vale! ¿Dónde quieres que nos veamos?
USTED Come to my house at 8 p.m. We'll have a drink and then decide where to go for dinner.
PACO ¿No crees que debiéramos reservar una mesa? Todos los restaurantes van a estar llenos.
USTED Perhaps you are right. Do you want me to make a reservation in a restaurant not far from where I live?
PACO Muy bien. Te lo dejo a ti. Nos vemos en tu casa. Adiós. Hasta el sábado.
USTED Goodbye, and thank you for ringing.

13

Exercise 7

Complete the following sentences using the appropriate idiom with the verb tener in the correct form:

1 Me voy a bañar en la piscina porque ….
2 No quería quedarse sola en casa porque ….
3 Se puso la chaqueta porque ….
4 Vamos a tomar una cerveza porque ….
5 Se acostaron temprano porque ….
6 No pudimos esperar más porque ….
7 Nos reímos mucho con la película porque ….
8 No comieron nada para el desayuno porque ….
9 No ganaré nunca la lotería porque ….

Exercise 8

Translate:

1 That coat doesn't fit you (fam. sing.) very well.
2 He has fallen ill and he has been taken to hospital.
3 We decided to go for a short walk.
4 Hurry up (fam. sing.) The train leaves at 9.45.
5 He never says good morning to me.
6 They started to go up the mountain, but they soon gave up.
7 I have come to say goodbye.
8 We cannot blame anybody.
9 You (fam. sing.) must miss Pedro, he was a good friend of yours.
10 Did you (pol. sing.) lock the suitcase before leaving the room?
11 I don't want you to contradict me.
12 We get on very well, we never argue.
13 It's better to take the umbrella, it may rain.

13

Exercise 9

Translate:

1 What a lot of people!
2 The man we saw yesterday is her husband.
3 Whose magazines are these?
4 Which seat do you (fam. sing.) prefer?
5 What a boring film!
6 The woman for whom she works is an actress.
7 How difficult it is to see him!
8 The room in which we slept overlooked the sea.
9 Those who need more information may ask that lady.
10 You (fam. sing.) must show me the present he has given you.
11 It is we who have to send it.
12 He didn't want to go, which surprised me.
13 I asked him who had come, but he didn't tell me.
14 That is the woman whose house they have bought.
15 They are friends with whom I am always in touch.
16 What we don't understand is why he hasn't written.

13

Reading practice

The following extracts from works by modern Spanish authors each have an English translation on the facing page. Refer to this as little as possible during your first reading of the Spanish, then go through the piece again, noting constructions and vocabulary.

Primera Memoria

—Te domaremos — me dijo mi abuela, apenas llegué a la isla.

Tenía doce años, y por primera vez comprendí que me quedaría allí para siempre. Mi madre murió cuatro años atrás y Mauricia – la vieja aya que me cuidaba – estaba impedida por una enfermedad. Mi abuela se hacía cargo definitivamente de mí, estaba visto.

El día que llegué a la isla, hacía mucho viento en la ciudad. Unos rótulos medio desprendidos tableteaban sobre las puertas de las tiendas. Me llevó la abuela a un hotel oscuro, que olía a humedad y lejía. Mi habitación daba a un pequeño patio, por un lado, y, por el otro, a un callejón, tras cuya embocadura se divisaba un paseo donde se mecían las palmeras sobre un pedazo de mar plomizo. La cama de hierro forjado, muy complicada, me amedrentó como un animal desconocido. La abuela dormía en la habitación contigua, y de madrugada me desperté sobresaltada – como me ocurría a menudo y busqué, tanteando, con el brazo extendido, el interruptor de la luz de la mesilla. Recuerdo bien el frío de la pared estucada, y la pantalla rosa de la lámpara. Me estuve muy quieta, sentada en la cama, mirando recelosa alrededor, asombrada del retorcido mechón de mi propio cabello que resaltaba oscuramente contra mi hombro. Habituándome a la penumbra, localicé, uno a uno, los desconchados de la pared, las grandes manchas del techo, y sobre todo, las sombras enzarzadas de la cama, como serpientes, dragones, o misteriosas figuras que apenas me atrevía a mirar. Incliné el cuerpo cuanto pude hacia la mesilla, para coger el vaso de agua, y entonces, en el vértice de la pared, descubrí una hilera de hormigas que trepaba por el muro. Solté el vaso, que se rompió al caer, y me hundí de nuevo entre las sábanas, tapándome la cabeza. No me decidía a sacar ni una mano, y así estuve mucho rato, mordiéndome los labios y tratando de ahuyentar las despreciables lágrimas. Me parece que tuve miedo. Acaso pensé que estaba completamente sola, y, como buscando algo que no sabía.

Taken from the novel *Primera Memoria* by Ana Maria Matute (born 1926).

First Memory

'We shall tame you,' my grandmother told me as soon as I arrived on the island.

I was twelve years old, and for the first time I realized that I would be staying there forever. My mother had died four years earlier and Mauricia, the old nanny who had looked after me, was now an invalid. My grandmother was going to take charge of me forever, that was clear.

The day I arrived on the island, it was very windy in the city. Some placards hanging loose were rattling on the doors of the shops. Grandmother took me to a gloomy hotel that smelt of dampness and bleach. My room overlooked a small yard on one side, and on the other side, an alley at the end of which one could see a promenade with palm trees swaying over a leaden sea. The intricate design of the wrought-iron bed frightened me like an unknown animal. Grandmother was sleeping in the room next to mine and at dawn I woke up startled, as I often did, and I stretched out my arm groping for the switch of the bedside lamp. I remember well the coldness of the stuccoed wall and the pink lampshade. I remained very still, sitting up in bed, looking around me suspiciously, fascinated by a curly lock of my hair resting darkly on my shoulder. As I got used to the dimness I noticed, one by one, the chips on the wall, the large stains on the ceiling and, above all, the twisted shadows of the bed, like snakes, dragons or mysterious figures that I hardly dared look at. I leant over to the bedside table, to pick up a glass of water, and then, in the corner of the room, I discovered a row of ants climbing up the wall. I dropped the glass, which broke, and sunk back between the sheets, covering my head. I did not dare show even one hand and I remained that way a long time, biting my lips and trying to hold back the despicable tears. I think I was afraid. Perhaps I thought that I was completely alone, and I was looking for something I did not know.

Los Españolitos de Alsemberg

A Santi se le hizo muy cuesta arriba vivir en la casa de los Dufour. Y no es que no le tratasen bien, no. Al contrario, tanto Raymond Dufour como su mujer, Arlette, hicieron desde el principio todo lo posible para que Santi se sintiese a sus anchas y para que no le faltase nada de cuanto podía necesitar o desear.

Durante varios días, Arlette y Raymond Dufour habían estado hablando de como sería el niño español que había de venir a su casa y era cosa decidida que ellos harían todo lo posible para tratarle con comprensión y cariño. Vivían en una casa amplia, muy bonita, de dos pisos, como un chalet, en el barrio de Forest, cerca de un parque lleno de flores y de campos de tenis y de fútbol, con pequeños tio-vivos y toboganes y columpios. Era un parque alegre y sonriente que estaba todo el día lleno de niños, de escolares, de niñeras y de palomas. Para Santi habían hecho empapelar y amueblar especialmente una habitación muy simpática, luminosa, con una pequeña chimenea, estanterías llenas de libros españoles y muchas pinturas y fotografías de España y banderines y juguetes.

Pero nada más entrar en la habitación, aquella primera noche, Santi supo que no se iba a encontrar a gusto. Se sintió emocionado al observar el cariño con que los Dufour habían preparado todo aquello para él y captó la mirada expectante de Madame Dufour que parecía preguntarse, con angustia, si aquello le gustaba o no.

Santi era cortés y tenía un gran sentido de gratitud. Dijo que todo era muy bonito y que gracias. Madame Dufour le abrazó y habló con su marido y Raymond Dufour dijo:

—Dice que quiere que seas feliz con nosotros, Santiago.

Ella le trajo un vaso de leche y unas galletas y aunque Santi no tenía ninguna gana de tomar nada, tomó el vaso de leche por complacerla. Las galletas no, porque realmente no podía.

La cama era cómoda y limpia. Raymond Dufour había depositado la maleta de Santi al lado de la cama y Santi no sabía qué hacer. Bostezó dos veces adrede – aunque estaba realmente muy cansado; las emociones del día le habían agotado – y Madame Dufour pronunció unas palabras en francés. Monsieur Dufour dijo:

—Duerme bien, Santiago. Mañana iremos de compras y también iremos en coche de paseo por Bruselas para que veas la ciudad. Luego almorzaremos en un restaurante, compras el regalo que quieras para tu hermana, e iremos a verla. ¿Te parece?

Los Españolitos de Alsemberg is taken from *El otro árbol de Guernica* (The other tree of Guernica) by Luis de Castresana (born 1925).

The Spanish Children of Alsemberg

Santi found it very hard to live in the Dufours' house. It wasn't that they did not treat him well. On the contrary, from the beginning both Raymond Dufour and his wife Arlette did all they could to make Santi feel at ease and to give him everything that he needed or wished.

For several days, Arlette and Raymond Dufour had been talking of what the little Spanish boy who was coming to their house might be like, and they decided that they would do everything in their power to treat him with understanding and love. They lived in a big, two-storey house, very pretty, like a villa, in the Forest district, near a park full of flowers, with tennis courts and a football pitch, with small roundabouts and slides and swings. It was a cheerful, jolly park which was always full of children, schoolboys, nannies and pigeons. They had had a room papered and furnished specially for Santi, a very pleasant, light room, with a small fireplace, bookshelves full of Spanish books and many pictures and photographs of Spain and pennants and toys.

But as soon as Santi entered the room, that first night, he knew that he wasn't going to feel happy there. He was touched by the love with which the Dufours had prepared all that for him and he was aware of the expectant look of Madame Dufour, who seemed to be wondering, anxiously, whether he liked all that or not.

Santi was polite and he had a great sense of gratitude. He said that everything was very nice and he thanked them. Madame Dufour hugged him and spoke to her husband and Raymond Dufour said: 'She says that she wants you to be happy with us, Santiago'.

She brought him a glass of milk and some biscuits and although Santi didn't feel like having anything, he drank the milk just to please her. He didn't eat the biscuits, he really couldn't.

The bed was comfortable and clean. Raymond Dufour had left Santi's suitcase by the bed and Santi didn't know what to do next. He yawned twice on purpose – although he really was very tired; the emotions of the day had made him feel exhausted – and Madame Dufour said a few words in French. Monsieur Dufour said: 'Sleep well, Santiago. Tomorrow we shall go shopping and we shall also go for a ride in the car round Brussels so that you can see the city. Then we shall have lunch in a restaurant, you buy any present you like for your sister and we shall go to visit her. Does that suit you?'

El Coronel no tiene quien le escriba

El viernes siguiente volvió a las lanchas. Y como todos los viernes regresó a su casa sin la carta esperada. 'Ya hemos cumplido con esperar', le dijo esa noche su mujer. 'Se necesita tener esa paciencia de buey que tú tienes para esperar una carta durante quince años'. El coronel se metió en la hamaca a leer los periódicos.

—Hay que esperar el turno — dijo. — Nuestro número es el mil ochocientos veintitrés.

—Desde que estamos esperando, ese número ha salido dos veces en la lotería — replicó la mujer.

El coronel leyó, como siempre, desde la primera página hasta la última, incluso los avisos. Pero esta vez no se concentró. Durante la lectura pensó en su pensión de veterano. Diecinueve años antes, cuando el congreso promulgó la ley, se inició un proceso de justificación que duró ocho años. Luego necesitó seis años más para hacerse incluir en el escalafón. Esa fue la última carta que recibió el coronel.

Terminó después del toque de queda. Cuando iba a apagar la lámpara cayó en la cuenta de que su mujer estaba despierta.

—¿Tienes todavía aquel recorte?

La mujer pensó.

—Sí. Debe estar con los otros papeles.

Salió del mosquitero y extrajo del armario un cofre de madera con un paquete de cartas ordenadas por las fechas y aseguradas con una cinta elástica. Localizó un anuncio de una agencia de abogados que se comprometía a una gestión activa de las pensiones de guerra.

—Desde que estoy con el tema de que cambies de abogado ya hubiéramos tenido tiempo hasta de gastarnos la plata — dijo la mujer, entregando a su marido el recorte de periódico. — Nada sacamos con que nos la metan en el cajón como a los indios.

El coronel leyó el recorte fechado dos años antes. Lo guardó en el bolsillo de la camisa colgada detrás de la puerta.

—Lo malo es que para el cambio de abogado se necesita dinero.

—Nada de eso — decidió la mujer. — Se les escribe diciendo que descuenten lo que sea de la misma pensión cuando la cobren. Es la única manera de que se interesen en el asunto.

Así que el sábado en la tarde el coronel fue a visitar a su abogado.

Taken from the novel *El Coronel no tiene quien le escriba* by the Colombian author Gabriel García Márquez (born 1928).

No one writes to the Colonel

The following Friday he went down to the launches again. And, as on every Friday, he returned home without the long-awaited letter. 'We've waited long enough,' his wife told him that night. 'One must have the patience of an ox, as you do, to wait for a letter for fifteen years.' The colonel got into his hammock to read the newspapers.

'We have to wait our turn,' he said. 'Our number is 1823.'

'Since we've been waiting, that number has come up twice in the lottery,' his wife replied.

The colonel read, as usual, from the first page to the last, including the advertisements. But this time he didn't concentrate. During his reading, he thought about his veteran's pension. Nineteen years earlier, when Congress passed the law, it took him eight years to prove his claim. Then it took him six more years to get himself included on the rolls. That was the last letter the colonel had received.

He finished after curfew sounded. When he went to turn off the lamp, he realized that his wife was awake.

'Do you still have that clipping?'

The woman thought.

'Yes. It must be with the other papers.'

She got out of her mosquito netting and took a wooden box out of the wardrobe, with a bundle of letters arranged by dates and held together by a rubber band. She found the advertisement of a legal firm which promised quick action on war pensions.

'We could have spent the money in the time I've wasted trying to convince you to change lawyers,' the woman said, handing her husband the newspaper clipping. 'We won't get anything out of it if they put the money in our coffin as they do with the Indians.'

The colonel read the clipping dated two years before. He put it in the pocket of his jacket which was hanging behind the door.

'The problem is that to change lawyers you need money.'

'Not at all,' said the woman decisively. 'You write to them telling them to discount whatever it may be from the pension itself when they collect it. It's the only way they'll work with interest on the case.'

So, Saturday afternoon the colonel went to see his lawyer.

Un pueblo de sueño

Llegamos a Sevilla y fuimos a un hotel de una plaza con grandes palmeras.

Nos han instalado en habitaciones del piso bajo, cuyas ventanas dan a un gran patio con una fuente en medio, enlozado de mármol blanco, y rodeado de una arcada también de mármol.

El cuarto me ha parecido húmedo y frío, como sitio donde no entra el sol y que no tiene chimenea ni nada para calentarlo.

Mi marido y yo cenamos a las ocho, y después de cenar fuimos a dar una vuelta por el pueblo.

En la calle de las Sierpes he llamado la atención. ¿Por qué? Realmente no llevaba nada llamativo. Quizá encontraban en mí cierto aire exótico.

Dimos varias vueltas a esta calle estrecha tortuosa, y luego nos sentamos en un café.

Al extranjero que viene a Sevilla lo que le choca primero son los muchos hombres que andan por la calle y las pocas mujeres.

En España he oído decir que se considera a las mujeres de Sevilla como muy bonitas, pero a mí, si tengo que decir la verdad y juzgar por las de la calle, no me han llamada la atención. En el Norte y en Madrid he visto tipos más bellos y con el mismo carácter meridional.

Realmente, en España no hay gran diferencia entre la gente del Norte y la del Sur; no pasa como en Italia; aquí, por lo que veo, apenas se distingue un andaluz de un vascongado y un gallego de un catalán.

Desde la ventana del café veo, un poco cansada, como se agita la multitud de hombres que llenan la calle. Hay muchos que deben de ser toreros, porque llevan coleta como los chinos, una coleta pequeña retorcida para arriba que parece el rabito de un cerdo.

Entre algunas de estas caras anémicas, borrosas, de poca expresión, hay tipos de hombres altos, con aire enérgico, que me recuerdan las esculturas romanas del Museo de Florencia. Muchos se apoyan en las paredes en actitud de languidez y de pereza.

—¿Estás cansada o damos otro paseo? — me ha preguntado Juan.

—No, vamos.

Hemos salido del café. Son cerca de las diez de la noche y muchas tiendas están abiertas. Sigue el eterno ir y venir de la gente.

Taken and adapted from the novel *El mundo es ansí* by Pío Baroja (1872–1956).

A dream town

We arrived in Seville and went to a hotel in a square with big palm trees.

They put us in rooms on the ground floor, whose windows overlook a large inner court with a fountain in the middle, a white marble floor and surrounded by a marble arcade.

The room seemed to me damp and cold, a place where the sun never enters and which has no fireplace or anything to warm it up.

My husband and I had dinner at eight, and after dinner we went for a walk around the town.

In Sierpes Street people were looking at me. Why? I was not wearing anything showy. Perhaps they found something exotic about me.

We walked up and down this narrow, winding street, and then went to sit in a café.

The first thing that strikes the foreigner who comes to Seville is how many men there are in the streets and how few women.

I have heard in Spain that the women of Seville are very pretty, but if I am to tell the truth and judge from the ones in the streets, they don't appeal to me. I have seen in the North and in Madrid much better looking women, with the same Southern characteristics.

Indeed, in Spain there is no great difference between the people of the North and that of the South; not like in Italy; here, as far as I can see, one can hardly tell an Andalusian from a Basque and a Galician from a Catalan.

From the window of the café I watch, feeling a little tired, the crowds of men that fill the street. Many of them must be bullfighters because they wear a plait like the Chinese, a small plait turned upwards that looks like a pig's tail.

Among these anaemic, blurred, expressionless faces, there are some tall, energetic looking men, who remind me of the Roman sculptures in the Museum in Florence. Many others are leaning against the wall in an attitude of listlessness and indolence. 'Are you tired or shall we go for another walk?' Juan asked me. 'No, let's go.'

We leave the café. It's nearly ten o'clock and many shops are still open. The continuous to-ing and fro-ing of people goes on.

Key to exercises

Exercise 1: 1 los libros. 2 las casas. 3 las mujeres. 4 los hombres. 5 las calles. 6 las flores. 7 los jardines. 8 los coches. 9 las capitales. 10 las ciudades. 11 las luces. 12 las leyes.

Exercise 2: 1 los. 2 el. 3 las. 4 la. 5 el. 6 los. 7 el. 8 la. 9 el. 10 las. 11 el. 12 el.
(indefinite articles): 1 unos; 2 un; 3 unas; 4 una; 5 un; 6 unos; 7 un; 8 una; 9 un; 10 unas; 11 un; 12 un.

Exercise 3: 1 el libro. 2 la mesa. 3 los billetes. 4 unos árboles. 5 una cerveza. 6 el coche. 7 una ciudad. 8 unas luces. 9 el jardín. 10 una calle. 11 unas mujeres. 12 la estación.

Exercise 4: 1 tienen una casa. 2 no tenemos café. 3 el hombre tiene miedo. 4 tengo que trabajar. 5 ¿tienes un lápiz? 6 no tienen sed. 7 ¿tienen Vds. todo? 8 tengo calor. 9 tenemos que salir. 10 tiene un hijo.

Drill 1: 1 no, no tengo hambre. 2 no, no tenemos cerveza. 3 no, no tengo sed. 4 no, no tenemos calor. 5 no, no tengo frío. 6 no, no tenemos los libros. 7 no, no tenemos los billetes.

WEEK 2

Exercise 5: 1 a la iglesia 2 del idioma 3 al coche 4 a la mesa 5 de los árboles 6 a la casa 7 del hombre 8 de la ciudad 9 a la calle 10 del vino 11 al policía 12 de la estación

Exercise 6: 1 buenos. 2 encantadora. 3 útiles. 4 blancas. 5 barato. 6 larga. 7 altos. 8 interesantes. 9 americano. 10 alemana.

Exercise 7: 1 son. 2 está. 3 son. 4 es. 5 están. 6 está. 7 es. 8 es. 9 está. 10 estoy.

Exercise 8: 1 es italiana. 2 las manzanas están en la cocina. 3 el autobús está allí. 4 Madrid es la capital de España. 5 la chica es alta. 6 la casa está en la colina. 7 es peligroso fumar. 8 el café está demasiado dulce. 9 mañana es domingo. 10 están en la playa.

WEEK 3

Exercise 9: 1 ese coche es caro. 2 esos hombres son fuertes.
3 esa iglesia es muy vieja. 4 estos amigos son de Málaga.
5 esta mesa está ocupada. 6 ese hombre está libre. 7 este
ascensor está lleno. 8 esas uvas están agrias. 9 aquellos
libros son interesantes. 10 es aquella playa.

Exercise 10: 1 estos, ésos. 2 esa, aquélla. 3 estas, ésas.
4 ese, éste. 5 este, aquél. 6 esos, éstos. 7 este, ése. 8 ese,
éste. 9 estas, ésas. 10 este, aquél.

Exercise 11: 1 compro. 2 fuma. 3 Vd. bebe. 4 escribimos.
5 aprenden. 6 estudio. 7 hablas. 8 come. 9 vivimos.
10 suben. 11 aprendo. 12 bebe.

Exercise 12: 1 compra un periódico. 2 ¿bebe cerveza?
3 Pedro vive en Barcelona. 4 escribo a Conchita. 5 ¿estudias
inglés? 6 estos niños aprenden español. 7 come demasiado.
8 subimos la colina. 9 hablo inglés. 10 beben vino barato.

Exercise 13: 1 el pueblo en el que vivimos. 2 la mujer que
trabaja en la tienda. 3 el libro que tengo que leer.
4 la ciudad de la que estamos hablando. 5 es Pedro quien es
médico. 6 ¿de quién son estas cartas? 7 ¿qué revista está
comprando? 8 la casa que tiene una puerta verde.
9 la pluma con la que escribo. 10 ¿cuál es el número?

Drill 2: 1 sí, bebemos cerveza. 2 sí, como pan. 3 sí, vivimos
en Boston. 4 sí, soy médico. 5 sí, hablamos español.
6 sí, compro la revista.

Drill 3: 1 no, no vivo en Barcelona. 2 no, no fumamos.
3 no, no aprendo alemán. 4 no, no compramos los
periódicos. 5 no, no bebo vino. 6 no, no somos españoles.

Drill 4: 1 está comprando. 2 están bebiendo. 3 estoy
estudiando. 4 estamos comiendo. 5 está leyendo. 6 estamos
hablando. 7 está escribiendo. 8 están aprendiendo.
9 estoy subiendo.

WEEK 4

Exercise 14: 1 mi marido. 2 su hermano. 3 nuestra hermana. 4 su sobrino. 5 su tío. 6 mis padres. 7 tu mujer. 8 sus hijos. 9 su primo. 10 sus parientes.

Exercise 15: 1 la tuya. 2 el suyo. 3 el nuestro. 4 la suya. 5 la nuestra. 6 el mío. 7 la suya. 8 los vuestros. 9 la mía. 10 el suyo.

Exercise 16: 1 diez casas. 2 setenta y dos euros. 3 doscientas mujeres. 4 dieciséis cartas. 5 ciento treinta y cinco libros. 6 cuarenta y seis hoteles. 7 trescientas cincuenta y cuatro manzanas. 8 sesenta y ocho tiendas. 9 mil cuatrocientos hombres. 10 setecientos ochenta y cinco coches.

Exercise 17: 1 el séptimo libro. 2 la primera mujer. 3 la tercera hija. 4 el sexto hijo. 5 la segunda puerta. 6 el décimo día.7 la cuarta calle. 8 el noveno niño. 9 el quinto hombre. 10 la octava tienda.

Exercise 18: 1 ¿qué hora es? 2 son las diez y veinte en mi reloj. 3 trabajo hasta las once y media. 4 el invierno en Madrid es frío. 5 tienen sus vacaciones en julio. 6 mi cumpleaños es el tres de enero. 7 está libre los sábados. 8 octubre es generalmente un mes bonito. 9 tenemos que ir a Barcelona en mayo. 10 los domingos ceno con mis padres.

REVISION EXERCISES 1

Exercise 1: 1 tengo. 2 viven. 3 es. 4 están. 5 comen. 6 habla. 7 son. 8 cena. 9 aprende. 10 trabajamos.

Exercise 2: 1 en España los periódicos americanos son muy caros. 2 ¿dónde están las maletas? 3 la habitación está en el tercer piso. 4 en el verano viven en Inglaterra y en el invierno viven en España. 5 su marido está enfermo, bebe demasiado. 6 tengo que escribir a mi amiga alemana. 7 estas flores son para la madre de Juan. 8 la Sra. Suárez es una mujer encantadora. 9 tenemos que comprar los billetes. 10 ¿qué hora es? son las siete y cuarto. 11 ¿es ese perro suyo? 12 nuestra hija está aprendiendo español.

Exercise 3: 1 soy americano(a). 2 no, vivo en Boston.
3 estoy de vacaciones. 4 sólo dos. 5 sí, trabajo en una tienda.
6 es una librería. 7 no, estoy en casa de una amiga. 8 en una
casa en la playa. 9 no, gracias, tengo prisa. Adiós.

WEEK 5

Exercise 19: 1 vamos a la iglesia los domingos. 2 voy a
comprar ese libro. 3 va a casa de su amigo. 4 vamos de
vacaciones en el verano. 5 van a Madrid en tren. 6 vamos a
tomar un café. 7 no va a cantar. 8 mañana voy a descansar.
9 van de compras en el mercado. 10 vamos al teatro.

Exercise 20: 1 he escrito tres cartas. 2 han hablado en
español. 3 hemos comido demasiado. 4 hay azúcar en este té.
5 ha comprado un vestido nuevo. 6 ¿has terminado el trabajo?
7 nunca ha ayudado en la casa. 8 hay unas naranjas en la
bolsa. 9 ¿ha bebido Vd. la cerveza? 10 no he visto la película.

Exercise 21: 1 a. 2 a. 3 –. 4 al. 5 –. 6 a. 7 –. 8 –. 9 –. 10 a.

Exercise 22: 1 visita a su madre. 2 he visto a la mujer.
3 tenemos que llamar a los perros. 4 María prepara la
comida. 5 han invitado a sus amigos. 6 tiene una hermana
casada. 7 voy a comprar un caballo. 8 tenemos que bañar
al niño. 9 están esperando al profesor. 10 Carlos no ha
visto Toledo.

Exercise 23: 1 Juan se lo ofrece. 2 la bebo por la mañana.
3 lo hemos comprado. 4 me las ha enviado. 5 se la he escrito.
6 los comemos. 7 estos señores no lo comprenden. 8 tengo
que estudiarla. 9 nos las ha vendido. 10 se los hemos dado.

Exercise 24: 1 no fume Vd. 2 beba Vd. este vino.
3 envíeme Vd. la revista. 4 léales Vd. la carta. 5 véndale Vd.
su reloj. 6 aprenda Vd. estos números. 7 escriba Vd. su
nombre aquí. 8 no coma Vd. esas manzanas. 9 no compre
Vd. esa carne. 10 no me los dé Vd.

Exercise 24 (plurals): 1 no fumen Vds. 2 beban Vds.
3 envíenme Vds. 4 léanles Vds. 5 véndanle Vds. 6 aprendan

Vds. 7 escriban Vds. 8 no coman Vds. 9 no compren Vds.
10 no me los den Vds.

Drill 5: 1 no, voy a tomarla ahora. 2 no, van a ir ahora.
3 no, va a escribirla ahora. 4 no, vamos a hacerlo ahora.
5 no, voy a comprarlos ahora. 6 no, van a verle ahora.
7 no, vamos a terminarla ahora. 8 no, va a llamarla ahora.
9 no, voy a subirlas ahora. 10 no, vamos a beberlo ahora.

Drill 6: 1 sí, cómprelo. 2 sí, súbanlas. 3 sí, llámele.
4 sí, invítenles. 5 sí, léala. 6 sí, envíenlas. 7 sí, bébala.
8 sí, véndanla.

Drill 7: 1 ya lo he preparado. 2 ya le hemos llamado.
3 ya lo he escrito. 4 ya la hemos tomado. 5 ya los he
comprado. 6 ya les hemos hablado. 7 ya los he contado.
8 ya lo hemos vendido. 9 ya la he leído.

WEEK 6

Exercise 25: 1 Pedro y Anita se escriben todos los días.
2 el coche va a pararse. 3 vamos a casarnos. 4 los niños se
acuestan a las ocho. 5 tenemos que lavarnos. 6 los dos
hombres se odian. 7 siempre me pide dinero. 8 nunca se
ayudan. 9 Carlos vuelve de la oficina a las seis y media.
10 tengo que dormirme. 11 llévese Vd. estas tazas.
12 la calle se llama Baeza. 13 voy a sentarme aquí.
14 nos vamos mañana. 15 me he decidido a vivir en España.

Exercise 26: 1 estamos trabajando con ellos. 2 ha comprado
un regalo para mí. 3 ¿va a volver con Vd.? 4 el tiempo está
contra nosotros. 5 se han ido sin él. 6 siempre ha vivido
conmigo. 7 estas cartas son para ella. 8 van a comprar la
casa entre ellos. 9 ¿están los niños contigo? 10 según él, el
viaje es demasiado largo.

Exercise 27: 1 ¿qué tiempo hace? 2 hoy hace mucho frío.
3 va a llover mañana. 4 no me gusta esta cerveza. 5 va a
traernos café. 6 le gusta salir todas las tardes. 7 no sé dónde
está. 8 van a España porque les gusta el sol. 9 hace
veinticinco años. 10 a Carmen le gusta sentarse en el jardín.

Drill 8: 1 sí, me gusta mucho. 2 sí, le gustan mucho. 3 sí, nos gusta mucho. 4 sí, nos gusta mucho. 5 sí, le gusta mucho. 6 sí, me gustan mucho. 7 sí, me gusta mucho. 8 sí, les gusta mucho. 9 sí, nos gusta mucho. 10 sí, les gusta mucho.

Drill 9: 1 sí, trabajo con ella. 2 sí, es para Vds. 3 sí, vuelve conmigo. 4 sí, vamos sin ellos. 5 sí, son para Vd. 6 sí, vive con ellos. 7 sí, son para nosotros. 8 sí, voy sin él.

Drill 10: 1 sí, quisiera sentarme. 2 sí, quisiera lavarme. 3 sí, quisiera dormirme. 4 sí, quisiera irme. 5 sí, quisiera pararme. 6 sí, quisiéramos sentarnos. 7 sí, quisiéramos lavarnos. 8 sí, quisiéramos dormirnos. 9 sí, quisiéramos irnos. 10 sí, quisiéramos pararnos.

WEEK 7

Exercise 28: 1 Luis vendía un coche. 2 generalmente la veo por la mañana. 3 habían hablado con el gerente del hotel. 4 solía traerme bombones. 5 el muchacho buscaba su maleta. 6 la representación solía empezar a las diez. 7 había trabajado en una fábrica. 8 el mar estaba muy frío. 9 la mujer nos miraba. 10 solíamos comer mucho pescado.

Exercise 29: 1 nada. 2 nadie. 3 ni, ni. 4 nunca. 5 ningún. 6 tampoco. 7 nadie. 8 nada. 9 ninguna. 10 nunca.

Exercise 30: 1 felizmente. 2 verdaderamente. 3 tristemente. 4 lentamente. 5 nuevamente. 6 agradablemente. 7 malamente. 8 ciertamente. 9 rápidamente. 10 claramente.

Exercise 31: 1 mi hermano es más fuerte que yo. 2 este jerez es más seco que ése. 3 Carlos es tres años mayor que María. 4 los zapatos negros son más pequeños que los azules. 5 su coche es mejor que el mío. 6 escribe peor que su hermana. 7 he llegado más pronto que mi padre. 8 no tienen tanto dinero como sus amigos. 9 no necesito tantas maletas como tú. 10 el agua en la piscina está más caliente que en el mar.

Drill 11: 1 sí, solía verla. 2 sí, solían comer. 3 sí, solíamos trabajar. 4 sí, solía escribirlas. 5 sí, solía viajar. 6 sí, solíamos ir.

7 sí, solía hablarlo. 8 sí, solía invitarles. 9 sí, solían tenerlo.
10 sí, solía beberlo.

Drill 12: 1 no, no quiero nada. 2 no, no han vivido aquí
nunca. 3 no, no queremos ni té ni café. 4 no, no hay ningún
turista inglés. 5 no, no conocemos a nadie. 6 no, no tengo
ninguna revista española.

Drill 13: 1 los míos son más viejos. 2 el mío es peor.
3 el mío es más bonito. 4 el mío es mejor. 5 el mío es más
alto. 6 los míos son más caros. 7 las mías son más grandes.
8 los míos son más baratos.

REVISION EXERCISES 2

Drill 1: 1 nos gusta más el vino. 2 nos gusta más la carne.
3 le gusta más la playa. 3 me gusta más el rugby. 5 les gusta
más jugar. 6 me gusta más Barcelona.

Exercise 1: 1 voy a una fiesta mañana y necesito un vestido
nuevo. 2 hemos visto una película muy buena en el 'Roxy'.
3 no puede venir a la playa con nosotros, tiene demasiado
trabajo. 4 Pedro es muy simpático, pero no tiene paciencia
con los niños. 5 la representación no empieza hasta las diez
y cuarto – es demasiado tarde para nosotros. 6 no han podido
salir porque ha llovido todo el día. 7 tenemos que esperar
hasta las cuatro y media porque las tiendas están cerradas.

Drill 2: 1 sí, lávelo. 2 no, no la espere. 3 sí, pregúntele.
4 no, no se las lleve. 5 sí, llámele. 6 no, no le invite.
7 sí, póngalas. 8 no, no lo haga.

Drill 3: 1 sí, termínenlo. 2 no, no lo pidan. 3 sí, véanla.
4 no, no se bañen. 5 sí, cómprenlos. 6 no, no la preparen.
7 sí, envíenlas. 8 sí, ayúdenle.

Exercise 2: 1 (d). 2 (g). 3 (f). 4 (h). 5 (c). 6 (a). 7 (e). 8 (b).

Exercise 3: • Pasado mañana es el cumpleaños de Luisa.
•¿Qué podemos comprarle? • Solo puedo pensar en
bombones, flores … • Lee mucho y le gusta viajar. ¿Por qué

no le compramos un libro de viajes? • Entonces, vamos decompras esta tarde y buscamos algo.

WEEK 8

Exercise 32: 1 hemos tenido un buen viaje. 2 cada hombre tenía un trabajo. 3 es un gran pintor. 4 siempre llevan la misma ropa. 5 hay bastantes hoteles en esta zona. 6 la pobre mujer ha perdido su bolsa. 7 tengo un sombrero nuevo. 8 hemos pedido otra bebida. 9 estos sellos son muy viejos. 10 todos los niños son buenos nadadores.

Exercise 33. 1 se casarán el próximo mes. 2 me acostaré temprano esta noche. 3 vendrá con nosotros de vacaciones. 4 les visitaremos el domingo. 5 no quieren hablar con nosotros. 6 sería mejor parar. 7 no me gustaría conducir un coche grande. 8 no tendrá que andar muy lejos. 9 no valdrían nada. 10 no podremos ver el museo. 11 no quería vender la casa. 12 el autocar saldrá a las ocho.

Exercise 34: 1 cierre Vd. las ventanas antes de acostarse. 2 tendré que pensar antes de decidir. 3 no puedes irte antes de terminar el trabajo. 4 ha pasado el día sin hablar con nadie. 5 lloraba sin saber por qué. 6 se sentían enfermos después de comer marisco. 7 tenía mucho sueño después de trabajar toda la noche. 8 nos gustaría ver la habitación antes de tomarla. 9 su voz estaba ronca de gritar tanto. 10 después de escribir la carta enséñemela Vd.

Drill 14: 1 no, le verán luego. 2 no, lo terminaremos luego. 3 no, iré luego. 4 no, la escribirá luego. 5 no, las enviaremos luego. 6 no, la cerrarán luego. 7 no, saldrá luego. 8 no, la haré luego. 9 no, las verán luego. 10 no, las abriré luego.

Drill 15: 1 hace seis meses que estudio español. 2 hace tres años que estamos en Madrid. 3 hace dos semanas que trabajan aquí. 4 hace un año que vive en Los Angeles. 5 hace diez minutos que espero. 6 llevo seis meses estudiando español. 7 llevamos tres años en Madrid. 8 llevan dos semanas trabajando aquí. 9 lleva un año viviendo en Los Angeles. 10 llevo diez minutos esperando.

Exercise 35: 1 dimos un paseo por el río. 2 no quisieron verme. 3 puse la carta en el sobre. 4 murió dos años después. 5 pagó la comida con un cheque. 6 el camarero nos trajo las bebidas y se fue. 7 anduvieron cinco kilómetros buscando un garaje. 8 salí a las diez y volví a la hora de comer. 9 le dijimos que su padre había llegado. 10 no hizo nada toda la mañana.

Exercise 36: 1 salió. 2 estaba, sonó. 3 viajaban, tuvieron. 4 jugaban, empezó. 5 bajó, hacía. 6 se sentaba. 7 volví. 8 hacía, llegamos. 9 recibió, vivía. 10 preguntó.

Exercise 37: 1 no conocen ese CD. 2 sabe que quiero un ordenador. 3 ese programa de televisión es divertidísimo. 4 esta talla es la más pequeña que tenemos. 5 estos zapatos son los más bonitos, ésos son los más baratos. 6 es el hombre más amable que conozco. 7 no saben que deseo verles. 8 fue una conversación interesantísima. 9 es la iglesia más vieja de esta ciudad. 10 la farmacia estaba lejos de la parada de autobús.

Exercise 38: 1 el té es una bebida muy agradable. 2 la señora Collado llegará el domingo. 3 se puso los guantes porque hacía frío. 4 él es camarero y ella es dependienta. 5 pasé dos semanas en el hospital. 6 lo importante es no preocuparse. 7 la pobre María se ha roto el brazo derecho. 8 los libros son muy caros hoy día. 9 andaba con gran dificultad. 10 va a traer otra taza. 11 bebimos media botella de coñac. 12 lo mejor es vender la casa.

Drill 16: 1 pero tuvo que escribirla. 2 pero tuvieron que pagarla. 3 pero tuve que verle. 4 pero tuvimos que ir. 5 pero tuvo que salir. 6 pero tuvo que hacerla. 7 pero tuvo que comerlo. 8 pero tuvo que fumarlo. 9 pero tuve que dárselo. 10 pero tuvimos que beberla.

Drill 17: 1 no, estuvimos ayer. 2 no, vinieron ayer. 3 no, lo compré ayer. 4 no, la pagaron ayer. 5 no, la recibió ayer. 6 no, las hicimos ayer. 7 no, llovió ayer. 8 no, las trajeron ayer. 9 no, fuimos ayer. 10 no, les visité ayer.

Drill 18: 1 sí, es el más bonito que he visto. 2 sí, son los más caros que he visto. 3 sí, es la más grande que he visto. 4 sí, es el más elegante que he visto. 5 sí, son los más divertidos que he visto. 6 sí, son las más pequeñas que he visto.

WEEK 10

Exercise 39: 1 por. 2 por. 3 para. 4 por. 5 para. 6 para. 7 por. 8 para. 9 para. 10 por.

Exercise 40: 1 tenemos que pasar por la Aduana. 2 nos cobraron diez euros por la comida. 3 es demasiado tarde para ir al cine. 4 necesito una bolsa para todas mis compras. 5 ¿tiene Vd. una llave para abrir este armario? 6 este libro es demasiado difícil para él. 7 el avión sale para Madrid a las siete y cuarto. 8 haría cualquier cosa por él. 9 leímos la carta por curiosidad. 10 quiere comprar unos melocotones para su madre.

Exercise 41: 1 la casa fue construida por su abuelo. 2 fui acusado del robo. 3 el barco se vendió por quinientos euros. 4 el trabajo está terminado ahora. 5 se cree que está muerto. 6 las montañas estaban cubiertas de nieve. 7 la cena no se sirve hasta las nueve. 8 las ventanas se pintaron hace tres semanas. 9 fueron recibidos por uno de los directores. 10 el programa fue presentado por un famoso actor.

Exercise 42: 1 jugué con los niños toda la tarde. 2 están construyendo un aparcamiento nuevo. 3 oyó un ruido arriba. 4 me sequé los pies al fuego. 5 cayeron al suelo. 6 está leyendo las instrucciones. 7 huyeron de España al principio de laguerra. 8 pagué mucho dinero por ese cuadro. 9 coja Vd. el equipaje, por favor. 10 creyó que la tienda estaba cerrada.

Exercise 43: 1 conseguí hablar con ellos. 2 nos aconsejó alquilar un coche. 3 trataron de entrar en la habitación. 4 pienso quejarme del servicio. 5 estamos aprendiendo a jugar al tenis. 6 volví a llamarle. 7 el señor Solís acaba de llegar. 8 se cansó de subir y se sentó. 9 dejó de llover y salió el sol. 10 me olvidé de darle el recado. 11 insistieron en pagar sus billetes. 12 el paquete tardó dos semanas en llegar.

13 acabaron por tener una discusión. 14 la mujer se esforzó por sonreír. 15 el hombre amenazó con llamar a la policía. 16 se contenta con ganar muy poco.

Drill 19: 1 para. 2 por. 3 para. 4 para. 5 por. 6 para. 7 para. 8 por.

Drill 20: 1 el libro se publicó. 2 los coches se alquilaron. 3 la puerta se abrió. 4 los ruidos se oyeron. 5 el trabajo se terminó. 6 la casa se construyó. 7 los barcos se vendieron. 8 la carta se leyó.

Drill 21: 1 sí, acabo de comprarlos. 2 sí, acaban de llegar. 3 sí, acabo de recibirlas. 4 sí, acabamos de hacerlas. 5 sí, acaban de acostarse. 6 sí, acabo de encontrarla.

REVISION EXERCISES 3

Exercise 1: 1 iremos. 2 cuidará. 3 trabajaré. 4 se levantará. 5 saldremos. 6 vendrá. 7 hará. 8 diré. 9 podrán. 10 tendrás.

Exercise 2: 1 traería. 2 volverían. 3 viajaría. 4 pagarían. 5 enviaría. 6 tendrían.

Exercise 3: 1 anoche vi a Antonio con su mujer. 2 el tren llegó dos horas tarde. 3 ofreció ayudarme con las bolsas. 4 no necesitamos ninguna ropa de invierno. 5 vendieron la casa a un amigo suyo. 6 conduje cien kilómetros sin parar. 7 fue a buscar una farmacia. 8 no le gustó el libro que le di.

Exercise 4: • Muy bien. Fue un viaje muy interesante. • Fuimos a Córdoba, Granada y Sevilla. • Mi mujer había estado en Sevilla, pero yo no conocía ninguna de ellas. • No sé. Es difícil elegir una. Cada una tiene una belleza diferente. Posiblemente Granada. La Alhambra es maravillosa. • Alberto, me gustaría seguir hablando, pero tengo que ir de compras con mi mujer. Estará esperándome. Te llamaré el viernes.

Exercise 5: 1 ¿por qué necesitas dinero? 2 lo necesito para comprar un coche nuevo. 3 salieron ayer para Venezuela. 4 estoy haciendo esto por ti. 5 estamos demasiado cansados para andar a la estación. 6 el hotel cuesta cinquenta euros por persona. 7 me ha invitado a su casa por un mes. 8 me enviaron una postal para decirme que venían.

Exercise 6: 1 se han cancelado los vuelos. 2 le acompañó su mujer. 3 se ha censurado la película. 4 se anunciaron las elecciones en octubre. 5 la policía arrestó al muchacho. 6 el Rey inauguró la exposición. 7 la explosión se oyó en todo el pueblo. 8 el banco no ha aceptado el cheque.

Exercise 7: 1 de, a. 2 a. 3 –. 4 a, de. 5 en. 6 a. 7 a. 8 –. 9 –. 10 de. 11 en. 12 –. 13 a. 14 –. 15 de. 16 con.

Exercise 8. 1 todos estamos cansados hoy. 2 mi hijo quiere ser abogado. 3 cuando estuvo enfermo, yo iba a visitarle todos los días. 4 no te sientes en esa silla, está rota. 5 hace mucho calor, aunque todas las ventanas están abiertas. 6 está triste porque su mejor amigo se ha muerto. 7 siempre estoy en casa los domingos. 8 es una mujer muy inteligente, pero no muy amable. 9 ¿quién es usted? soy un amigo suyo. 10 estábamos para salir cuando él llegó. 11 no le dieron el trabajo porque era demasiado joven. 12 éstas no son mis maletas, las mías son negras.

Exercise 9: 1 íbamos, nos quedábamos. 2 hizo, pidió. 3 tenía, podía. 4 llamó, estaba. 5 llevábamos, llegó. 6 fueron, volvieron, hacía. 7 llegué, estaba. 8 dejó, di. 9 salió, había. 10 trabajó, estaba.

WEEK 11

Exercise 44: 1 ¿cuánto le debo? 2 no deberían decir esas cosas. 3 debe de tener un buen trabajo. 4 debo ver a un médico. 5 ¿sabe hablar español? 6 no puedo leer sin gafas. 7 deberíamos ir allí más a menudo. 8 me debe una explicación. 9 esa sortija debe de costar mucho dinero. 10 no sé montar en bicicleta. 11 no puede dormir sin tomar píldoras. 12 ¿sabe Vd. guisar?

Exercise 45: 1 me alegro de que puedan venir. 2 quiere que el abogado vea los documentos. 3 nos han mandado que esperemos aquí. 4 dudo que salga el sol. 5 me sorprende que

no haya escrito. 6 me ha pedido que le enseñe español.
7 es posible que se hayan perdido. 8 es una lástima que no
tengamos bastante dinero. 9 es probable que se casen.
10 no podré hacerlo a no ser que me ayuden. 11 iremos al
cine con tal que me dejes pagar. 12 esperará hasta que yo
vuelva. 13 tendrán que comerlo, aunque no les guste.
14 no hay nadie que pueda pagar ese precio. 15 ¿hay
alguien que sepa tocar el piano? 16 necesito una mujer que
cuide de los niños. 17 lo encontraremos, dondequiera que
esté. 18 te ayudará cuandoquiera que tengas un problema.
19 por mucho que trate, nunca tendrá éxito. 20 por muy
fácil que parezca, se necesita práctica.

Exercise 46: 1 hazlo, no lo hagas. 2 ven, no vengas, venid.
3 acuéstate, no te acuestes. 4 aprende, no aprendas. 5 ponlo,
no lo pongas. 6 escríbela, no la escribas. 7 grita, no grites.
8 óyelo, no lo oigas. 9 preocúpate, no te preocupes.
10 duérmete, no te duermas.

Exercise 47: 1 no te enfades. 2 escuchadme. 3 vístete.
4 no me digáis eso. 5 tened cuidado. 6 léenoslo. 7 callaos.
8 no me despiertes temprano. 9 perdonad mi error.
10 no muevas el coche.

Drill 22: 1 sí, debe de estar enfermo. 2 sí, deben de ser las
cinco. 3 sí, deben de estar muy tristes. 4 sí, debe de trabajar
mucho. 5 sí, debe de hacer muchos años. 6 sí, deben de
estar en casa.

Drill 23: 1 sí, es preferible que coman. 2 sí, es preferible que
se vaya. 3 sí, es preferible que volvamos. 4 sí, es preferible
que se acuesten. 5 sí, es preferible que pague. 6 sí, es
preferible que nos sentemos.

Drill 24: 1 sí, pedidlos. 2 sí, tráelo. 3 sí, llamadle.
4 sí, cómpralo. 5 sí, abridlas. 6 sí, ayúdale.

Drill 25: 1 no, siguen comiendo. 2 no, sigue leyéndolo.
3 no, seguimos trabajando. 4 no, sigo pintando. 5 no, sigue
cantando. 6 no, siguen construyéndola.

Exercise 48: 1 querían que viajase con ellos. 2 tenía miedo de que hubiera tenido un accidente. 3 nos dijo que pusiéramos la mesa. 4 le pedí que se diera prisa. 5 esperábamos que no hiciese demasiado calor en Sevilla. 6 dondequiera que fuese, siempre encontraba amigos. 7 le avisé que no usara esa máquina. 8 me llamó por teléfono para que reservara las habitaciones. 9 buscaban a una persona que pudiese traducir la carta. 10 me alegro de que ganaran el primer premio.

Exercise 49: 1 lo haría si pudiera. 2 si hace buen tiempo, trabajaré en el jardín. 3 el perro no te habría mordido si no le hubieses pegado. 4 si les preguntaras, no sabrían que decir. 5 si le viera ahora, no le hablaría. 6 Vd. no habría perdido el dinero, si lo hubiera guardado en su bolsillo. 7 si vinieran a la fiesta, se divertirían. 8 te escribiré, si tengo que quedarme allí más tiempo. 9 si no llevas un paraguas, te mojarás. 10 yo iría al concierto, si él viniera conmigo.

Exercise 50: 1 ojalá no tuviera que trabajar. 2 quizá esté enfermo. 3 puede que haya perdido el tren. 4 que venga, si quiere. 5 ojalá pudiéramos tener unas vacaciones. 6 pase lo que pase, estaré en contacto con Vd. 7 ¿podemos ver las fotografías? 8 dijo que yo podía tener el día libre. 9 ¡que se divierta Vd! 10 quizá no vieran el aviso.

Exercise 51: 1 no te acerques al borde. 2 se asomó a la ventanilla del coche. 3 mi hermano va a casarse con una chica inglesa; 4 sabes que puedes contar conmigo. 5 la ventana daba a una calle muy concurrida. 6 el éxito de la obra depende de los actores. 7 tengo que despedirme de mis compañeros. 8 no dudan de su buena intención. 9 María se ha enamorado de un hombre muy tonto. 10 es muy fácil encontrarse con turistas americanas en España. 11 no hemos podido enterarnos de su nombre. 12 no me fijé en lo que llevaba. 13 tienes que ocuparte de las bebidas. 14 esta casa se parece mucho a la nuestra. 15 no quiere pensar en todos los problemas. 16 no sabemos lo que piensa de la situación. 17 este helado sabe a fresa. 18 soñaba con todos los lugares que había visitado.

Drill 26: 1 puede que lo venda. 2 puede que se casen.
3 puede que salgamos. 4 puede que vuelva. 5 puede que nos
inviten. 6 puede que nade.

Drill 27: 1 vendrían si pudieran. 2 lo pediríamos si lo
necesitáramos. 3 comería si tuviera hambre. 4 se lo diríamos
si le viéramos. 5 saldrían si no lloviera. 6 te lo daría si lo
encontrara. 7 trabajaría más si le pagaran bien. 8 hablaría
con ellos si vinieran.

Drill 28: 1 se sorprendió al oír la noticia. 2 gritaron al ver a
los policías. 3 lloraba al leer la carta. 4 me pidió la llave al
salir. 5 tuve miedo al oír un ruido. 6 se lavaron las manos al
terminar. 7 me quité el sombrero al entrar. 8 empezó a
llover al llegar a casa.

WEEK 13

Exercise 52: 1 mucha gente asistió al entierro. 2 esta
cantidad de harina bastará. 3 esa caja no cabe en el maletero.
4 quiero devolver la revista que me prestó. 5 echó la pelota
a los niños. 6 voy a echar el vino. 7 les falta experiencia.
8 faltan cinco libros de este estante. 9 nos hacen falta más
ayudantes. 10 meterán toda la ropa en una maleta.
11 ¿cuántos días te quedan? 12 quitará estas sillas.
13 ¿puedo quitarme la chaqueta? 14 sobran huevos para
hacer la tortilla. 15 es muy agradable tocar seda.
16 le gustaría tocar el violín. 17 tomó la pluma y firmó la
carta. 18 les gusta tomar vino con su comida.

Exercise 53: 1 ha heredado más de un millón de euros.
2 no puedo venderlo por menos de cien euros. 3 hemos
vivido en Madrid más de quince años. 4 lo haré en menos
de cinco minutos. 5 nunca había visto un collar tan bonito.
6 ¡qué edificio tan feo! 7 no haría tal cosa. 8 encuentro tales
libros muy aburridos. 9 ese no es mi hermano, sino mi
primo. 10 no tienen un perro, pero tienen dos gatos.
11 tiene más dinero de lo que dice. 12 son más listos de lo
que crees. 13 ¡qué idea tan buena! 14 ¡es un viaje tan largo!

Exercise 54: 1 el hombre dormía bajo un árbol. 2 me
escribió desde Córdoba. 3 después del teatro, fuimos a su
casa. 4 es muy espléndido con sus amigos. 5 esperamos a la

puerta, pero no vino. 6 según su padre, está muy enfermo.
7 había un fila larga de coches delante de mí. 8 tuvo que
presentarse ante el juez. 9 se fueron sin pagar la bebida.
10 puso la maleta debajo de la cama. 11 hay una zapatería
enfrente de la panadería. 12 no te veré hasta el domingo.
13 el ascensor se paró entre los dos pisos. 14 quiero probarlo
antes de comprarlo. 15 empezaremos a andar hacia la
estación. 16 tendrán que ir en el autobús. 17 el libro ha caído
detrás del sofá. 18 dejaré el paquete encima del escritorio.

Drill 29: 1 no, no le hace falta. 2 no, no nos hace falta.
3 no, no me hacen falta. 4 no, no les hace falta. 5 no, no le
hacen falta. 6 no, no nos hace falta.

Drill 30: 1 no podemos devolverlo todavía. 2 no puedo
meterla todavía. 3 no pueden echarlas todavía. 4 no puedo
quitármelos todavía. 5 no podemos tomarlo todavía.
6 no puede pagarla todavía.

Drill 31: 1 hasta. 2 desde. 3 enfrente de. 4 encima de.
5 entre. 6 sin. 7 con. 8 antes de. 9 en. 10 hacia.

REVISION EXERCISES 4

Exercise 1: 1 deben de haber salido. 2 no sabía ni leer, ni
escribir. 3 deberíamos esperar unos minutos más. 4 ¿puede
usted decirme la hora? 5 tenía miedo porque no sabía nadar.
6 deberías invitarla a cenar. 7 me deben doce euros. 8 debéis
decidir lo que queréis hacer.

Exercise 2: 1 vayamos. 6 ayude. 3 se queden. 4 salga.
5 sepa. 6 pueda. 7 llueva. 8 tengáis. 9 juegue. 10 llegues.
11 veamos. 12 venga. 13 llame. 14 tengan. 15 haga.
16 acompañe.

Exercise 3: 1 espera. 2 siéntate. 3 dale. 4 haz. 5 pidas. 6 ten.
7 traigas. 8 ven.

Exercise 4: 1 limpiad. 2 volváis. 3 comed. 4 acostaos.
5 le digáis. 6 vayáis. 7 escribíd. 8 me telefoneéis.

Exercise 5: 1 estuviera / estuviese. 2 enviara / enviase.

3 perdonáramos / perdonásemos. 4 fuera / fuese. 5 supiéramos
/ supiésemos. 6 pudieras / pudieses. 7 firmaran / firmasen.
8 hiciera / hiciese. 9 fuera / fuese. 10 necesitaras / necesitases.
11 vendiéramos / vendiésemos. 12 trajera / trajese.

Exercise 6: • Ya lo sé. He tenido mucho trabajo. • Lo siento.
No tengo ninguna noche libre esta semana. • ¿El sábado de la
semana próxima? • Ven a mi casa a las ocho. Tomaremos un
aperitivo y luego decidiremos adónde ir a cenar. • Quizás tengas
razón. ¿Quieres que haga una reserva en un restaurante no
lejos de donde vivo? • Adiós y gracias por llamar.

Exercise 7: 1 tengo calor. 2 tenía miedo. 3 tenía frío.
4 tenemos sed. 5 tenían sueño. 6 teníamos prisa. 7 tenía
gracia. 8 no tenían hambre. 9 no tengo suerte.

Exercise 8: 1 ese abrigo no te cae muy bien. 2 ha caído
enfermo y le han llevado al hospital. 3 decidimos dar un
paseo corto. 4 ¡date prisa! el tren sale a las diez menos cuarto.
5 nunca me da los buenos días. 6 empezaron a subir la
montaña, pero pronto se dieron por vencidos. 7 he venido a
despedirme. 8 no podemos echar la culpa a nadie. 9 debes
de echar de menos a Pedro, era un buen amigo tuyo.
10 ¿echó usted la llave a la maleta antes de salir de la
habitación? 11 no quiero que me lleves la contraria.
12 nos llevamos muy bien, nunca discutimos. 13 más vale
llevar el paraguas. es posible que llueva.

Exercise 9: 1 ¡cuánta gente! 2 el hombre que vimos ayer es
su marido. 3 ¿de quién son estas revistas? 4 ¿qué asiento
prefieres? 5 ¡qué película tan aburrida! 6 la mujer para
quien trabaja es actriz. 7 ¡qué difícil es verle! 8 la habitación
en la que dormimos daba al mar. 9 los que necesiten más
información, pueden preguntar a esa señora. 10 tienes que
enseñarme el regalo que te ha dado. 11 somos nosotros
quienes tenemos que enviarlo. 12 no quiso ir, lo cual me
sorprendió. 13 le pregunté quién había venido, pero no me
lo dijo. 14 esa es la mujer cuya casa han comprado.
15 son amigos con quienes siempre estoy en contacto.
16 lo que no comprendemos es por qué no ha escrito.

Mini-dictionary

The translations given are those which are found in the course; a full dictionary will list alternatives. In the Spanish–English section the article indicates the noun's gender. Adjectives are given in the masculine singular, followed by the endings for the feminine and plural. Remember that **CH**, **LL**, and **Ñ** are separate letters in Spanish and are listed separately in the dictionary. Thus **mañana** is found after **manzana**.

SPANISH–ENGLISH

a at, to, in ...
el abogado lawyer
el abrigo coat
abril April
abrir to open
aburrido (-a/-os/-as) boring
el abuelo grandfather
acabar to finish
acaso perhaps
el accidente accident
aceptar to accept
acercarse to approach
acompañar to accompany
aconsejar to advise
acordarse (de) to remember
acostarse to go to bed
el actor actor
la actriz actress
acusar to accuse
adiós goodbye
adonde where to
la Aduana Customs
el aeropuerto airport
la agencia de viajes travel agent's
agosto August
agradable pleasant
agrio (-a/-os/-as) sour
el agua water
ahora now
ahorrar to save (money/time)
alegrarse to be glad
alemán (alemana/-es/-as) German
al fuego by the fire
algo something
alguien someone, somebody
alguno (-a/-os/-as) some, any

alquilar to hire
alto (-a/-os/-as) tall
el alumno pupil
allí there
amable kind
amanecer to dawn
amenazar to threaten
a menudo often
el amigo friend
andar to walk
anochecer to get dark
ante before
antes de before
anunciar to announce
el año year
el aparcamiento car park
el aperitivo aperitif, drink
aprender to learn
apresar to seize
aquel (-la/-los/-las) that/those
   (over there)
el armario cupboard, wardrobe
el árbol tree
el arquitecto architect
arrancar to start (a car)
arrestar to arrest
arriba upstairs
el ascensor lift, elevator
así (que) thus, so
el asiento seat
asistir to assist, to attend
asomarse to lean out
el autobús bus
el autocar coach
el automóvil car
el avión aeroplane

avisar to warn
el aviso warning (sign)
el ayudante helper
ayudar to help
ayudarse to help each other
el azúcar sugar
azul blue

bailar to dance
el baile dance, dancing
bajar to go down
bajo under
la bala bullet
el banco bank
bañar to bath
bañarse to bathe (oneself)
el baño bathroom
barato (-a/-os/-as) cheap
la barca rowing boat
el barco boat, ship
bastante enough, fairly
bastar to suffice, to be enough
beber to drink
la bebida drink
la bicicleta bicycle
bien well
el billete ticket, note (money)
el bocadillo sandwich
la boda wedding
la bolsa bag
el bolsillo pocket
el bolso handbag
blanco (-a/-os/-as) white
los bombones chocolates
bonito (-a/-os/-as) pretty
el borde edge
la botella bottle
el brazo arm
la buena intención goodwill
bueno (-a/-os/-as) good
buscar to look for

el caballo horse
caber to fit in
cada each
el café coffee
la caja box

el cajón drawer
caliente hot, warm
el calor heat
callarse to be quiet
la calle street
la cama bed
el camarero waiter
el cambio change
el camino way
el camión lorry
la camisa shirt
el camisón nightdress
el campo country(side)
cancelar to cancel
cansado (-a/-os/-as) tired
cansarse to get tired
cantar to sing
la cantidad amount
la capital capital
la carne meat
la carnicería butcher's shop
caro (-a/-os/-as) expensive
la carretera road
la carta letter
la casa house, home
casado (-a/-os/-as) married
casarse to get married
casi almost
castigar to punish
la casualidad coincidence
la catedral cathedral
celebrar to celebrate
la cena dinner
cenar to have dinner
censurar to censor
cerca near
las cerillas matches
cerrar to close
la cerveza beer
ciego (-a/-os/-as) blind
cierto (-a/-os/-as) certain
el cigarrillo cigarette
el cine cinema
la ciudad city, town
claro of course
el cliente client
el clima climate

cobrar to charge
el coche car
la cocina kitchen
el colegio school
la colina hill
el color colour
el collar necklace
el comedor dining room
comer to eat
la comida meal, food, lunch
como how, as, like
el compañero colleague,
  companion
la compañía de seguros insurance
  company
comprar to buy
las compras purchases, shopping
comprender to understand
comprenderse to understand
  each other
con with
el concierto concert
concurrido busy, crowded
conducir to drive
conocer to know
conseguir to obtain, to manage
consentir to consent
conservador conservative
construir to build
el contable accountant, book-keeper
el contacto contact
contar to count
contentarse to content oneself
contento (-a/-os/-as) happy, pleased
contestar to answer
contra against
la conversación conversation
el coñac brandy
la corbata (neck-)tie
correcto (-a/-os/-as) correct, right
el correo post, mail
la cosa thing
la costa coast
costar to cost
la costumbre custom, habit
creer to believe
el cuadro picture

cual which
cualquier cosa anything
cuando when
cuanto how much
el cuarto room, fourth, quarter
cubierto (-a/-os/-as) covered
la cuenta bill
cuidar to look after
la culpa blame, fault
el cumpleaños birthday
la curiosidad curiosity

la chaqueta jacket
el cheque cheque
la chica girl

el daño damage, injury
dar to give
darse prisa to hurry
dar un paseo to go for a walk
de of, from
debajo (de) under, underneath
deber must, to owe
decidir to decide
decidirse a to decide
décimo (-a/-os/-as) tenth
decir to say
dejar(se) to let, to allow, to leave
  behind
delante (de) in front
delicioso (-a/-os/-as) lovely,
  delicious
demasiado too, too much
demasiado (-a/-os/-as) too much,
  too many
depender to depend
la dependienta shop girl
el deporte sport
derecho right
el desastre disaster
el desayuno breakfast
descansar to have a rest
describir to describe
desde from
desear to wish, to want
despacio slowly
el despacho office

despertar to waken
despertarse to wake up
despedir to dismiss
despedirse to say goodbye
después (de) after
detrás (de) behind
devolver to return, to give back
el día day
el día libre day off
diciembre December
difícil difficult
dificultad difficulty
diligentemente diligently
el dinero money
directamente straight
el director director
el disco record, disc
la discusión argument
discutir to argue
disparar to shoot
dispuesto ready
divertido amusing
divertirse to have a good time
el documento document
el domingo Sunday
dormir to sleep
dormirse to go to sleep
el dormitorio bedroom
la ducha shower
dudar to doubt
dudoso (-a/-os/-as) doubtful
dulce sweet
durante during
durar to last

echar to throw, to pour
el edificio building
el the
empezar to begin
el empleado employee
en in
enamorarse to fall in love
encantado (-a/-os/-as) delighted
encantador charming
encima (de) on top of
encontrar to find

encontrarse con to meet, to come across
enero January
enfadarse to get angry
enfermo (-a/-os/-as) ill
enfrente de opposite
enseñar to show, to teach
enterarse to find out
el entierro funeral
entonces then, in that case
entrar to come in
entre between
enviar to send
el equipaje luggage
el error error
escoger to choose
escribir to write
el escritorio desk
escuchar to listen
la escuela school
ese (-a/-os/-as) that, those
esforzarse to make an effort
España Spain
esperar to wait, to expect, to hope
espléndido generous
esta noche tonight
la estación station, season
el estante shelf
estar to be
estar en contacto con to be in touch with
este (-a/-os/-as) this, these
estudiar to study
el estudiante student
estupendo (-a/-os/-as) fine
estúpido (-a/-os/-as) stupid
el euro euro
el éxito success
la explicación explanation

la fábrica factory
fácil easy
fácilmente easily
faltar to lack, to be missing
famoso (-a/-os/-as) famous
farmacia chemist's shop
el fax fax

febrero February
la fecha date
feliz happy
feo (-a/-os/-as) ugly
la fiesta party
fijarse en to notice
la fila line, row
el fin end
firmar to sign
la flor flower
la fotografía photograph
francés (francesa/-es/-as) French
la fresa strawberry
frecuentemente frequently
fresco (-a/-os/-as) fresh
frío (-a/-os/-as) cold
fuerte strong
fuerza de voluntad willpower
fumar to smoke
la función performance

las gafas glasses
la galleta biscuit
ganar to earn, to win
la gasolina petrol
el gasto expense
el gato cat
generalmente usually
la gente people
el gerente manager
la ginebra gin
las gracias thanks
grande big
grave serious, grave
gritar to shout
el guante glove
guardar to keep
el guardia policeman
la guerra war
guisar to cook
gustar to like
el gusto pleasure

haber to have
la habitación room
hablar to speak, to talk
hacer to do, to make

hacer la maleta to pack (suitcase)
hacia towards
el hambre hunger
harina flour
hasta until
el helado ice cream
helar to freeze
heredar to inherit
la herida injury
la hermana sister
el hermano brother
la hija daughter
el hijo son
la historia history
hola hello
holgazán (holagazana/-es/-as) lazy
el hombre man
la hora hour, time
la hora de comer lunch time
horrible horrible
el hospital hospital
el hotel hotel
hoy today
hoy día nowadays
el huevo egg
huir to run away

la idea idea
el idioma language
la iglesia church
las ilustraciones illustrations
importante important
importar to matter
inaugurar to inaugurate
increíble incredible
inglés (inglesa/-es/-as) English
insistir to insist
insoportable unbearable
las instrucciones instructions
insultar to insult
inteligente intelligent
intentar to try to
interesante interesting
interesar to interest
el invierno winter
invitar to invite
ir to go

ir de compras to go shopping
ir de vacaciones to go on holiday
irse to go away
italiano (-a/-os/-as) Italian

jamás never
el jardín garden
el jerez sherry
joven young
el jueves Thursday
el juez judge
jugar to play
jugar (a) to play a game
julio July
junio June
juntos together
justo (-a/-os/-as) just

el kilómetro kilometre

la(-s) the
el ladrón thief, burglar
el lápiz pencil
largo (-a/-os/-as) long
la lástima pity
lavar to wash
lavarse to wash oneself
la leche milk
leer to read
lejos far
lento (-a/-os/-as) slow
levantarse to get up
leve minor
la ley law
libre free
el libro book
listo (-a/-os/-as) clever
Londres London
los the (plural)
el lugar place
el lunes Monday
la luz light

llamar to call
llamarse to call oneself, to be called
la llave key
llegar to arrive

lleno (-a/-os/-as) full
llevar to wear, to carry
llevarse to take away
llorar to cry
llover to rain

la madre mother
mal badly
la maleta suitcase
el maletero car boot
mandar to order
la manifestación demonstration
la mano hand
la manzana apple
mañana tomorrow
el mapa map
la máquina machine
el mar sea
maravillosamente wonderfully
el marido husband
el marisco seafood
el martes Tuesday
marzo March
más more
más tiempo longer
mayo May
la medianoche midnight
el médico doctor
medio (-a/-os/-as) half
mejor better
mejorar to get better
el melocotón peach
menos less
el mercado market
el mes month
la mesa table
meter to put in
mientras while
el miércoles Wednesday
mirar to look
mismo (-a/-os/-as) same
mojarse to get wet
molestar to bother, to trouble
el momento moment
la montaña mountain
montar en bicicleta to ride a bicycle
morder to bite

morir, morirse to die
el motor engine, motor
mover to move
la muchacha girl
el muchacho boy
mucho much, a lot
mucho (-a/-os/-as) much, a lot, many
muerto (-a/-os/-as) dead
la mujer wife, woman
la multa fine (penalty)
el museo museum
la música music
muy very

nada nothing
el nadador swimmer
nadie no one, nobody
la naranja orange
la neblina mist
necesitar to need
negro (-a/-os/-as) black
nevar to snow
ni ... ni neither ... nor
la niebla fog
la nieve snow
ninguno (-a/-os/-as) none
la niña girl
el niño boy
el nombre name
el norte north
la noticia news
la novela novel
noviembre November
nuevo (-a/-os/-as) new
el número number
nunca never

o or
o ... o either ... or
obedecer to obey
la obra (de teatro) play
octavo (-a/-os/-as) eighth
octubre October
ocupado (-a/-os/-as) occupied, taken, busy
ocuparse de to attend to

ocurrir to happen
odiar to hate
odiarse to hate each other
la oficina office
ofrecer to offer
oír to hear
el olor smell
olvidar(se) to forget
el ordenador computer
el oro gold
el otoño autumn
otro (-a/-os/-as) other

la paciencia patience
el padre father
los padres parents
pagar to pay
la palabra word
el pan bread
la panadería bakery
el panecillo bread roll
los pantalones trousers
el paquete parcel
para for
la parada de autobús bus stop
el paraguas umbrella
parar, pararse to stop
parecer to seem
los parientes relatives
pasado (-a/-os/-as) past, last
pasar to spend (time), to pass
pedir to ask for, to order
pegar to hit
la película film
peligroso (-a/-os/-as) dangerous
la pelota ball
pensar to think
peor worse
pequeño (-a/-os/-as) small, little
perder to lose, to miss (train, boat)
perderse to lose one's way
perdonar to forgive
el periódico newspaper
permitir to allow
pero but
el perro dog
la persona person

pertenecer to belong
el pescado fish (as food)
el pez fish (generic)
el piano piano
el pie foot
la pierna leg
la píldora pill
pintar to paint
el pintor painter
la piscina swimming pool
el piso floor, flat (apartment)
el pitillo cigarette
la playa beach
la pluma pen
pobre poor
poco little (amount)
poco (-a/-os/-as) little, few
poder to be able
la policía police
el policía policeman
poner to put
poner la mesa to lay the table
ponerse to put on
por by, along
la portezuela car door
la posibilidad possibility
la práctica practice
el precio price
preguntar to ask
el premio prize
preocuparse to worry
preparar to prepare
presentar to introduce
presentarse to appear, turn up
el presidente president
prestar to lend
la prima cousin (female)
la primavera spring (season)
primero (-a/-os/-as) first
el primo cousin (male)
principal main
el principio beginning
probar to try, to test
el problema problem
el profesor teacher
el programa programme
prohibir to forbid

prometer to promise
pronto soon
protestante protestant
provocar to provoke
próximo (-a/-os/-as) next
publicado published
el pueblo village
la puerta door
la pulsera bracelet

que what, who, which, that
quedar to remain, to have left
quedarse to stay
quejarse to complain
querer to want, to love
quererse to love each other
quien who, whom
¿quién? who?, whom?
las quinielas football pools
quinto (-a/-os/-as) fifth
quitar to take away, remove
quitarse to take off (clothes)
quizá(s) perhaps

rápido (-a/-os/-as) fast
la razón reason
razonable reasonable
la rebaja reduction
el recado message
recibir to receive
recoger to pick up
recordar to remember
el regalo present
la reina queen
reírse to laugh
el reloj watch, clock
la representación performance
reservar to book
el resultado result
el retraso delay
la revista magazine
rico (-a/-os/-as) rich, wealthy
el río river
el robo theft
romper, romperse to break
ronco (-a/-os/-as) hoarse
la ropa clothes

roto (-a/-os/-as) broken
el ruido noise
ruso (-a/-os/-as) Russian
el sábado Saturday
saber to know
saber a to taste of
el sacrificio sacrifice
salir to go out
el salón living room, lounge
saludar to greet
secar to dry
secarse to dry oneself
seco (-a/-os/-as) dry
la sed thirst
la seda silk
seguir to follow, to go on
según according to
segundo (-a/-os/-as) second
el sello postage stamp
la semana week
semejante such
sentarse to sit down
sentirse to feel
las señas address
el señor sir, Mr., gentleman
la señora madam, Mrs., lady
la señorita Miss, young lady
septiembre September
séptimo (-a/-os/-as) seventh
ser to be
el servicio service
servir to serve
severamente severely
sexto (-a/-os/-as) sixth
siempre always
el silencio silence
la silla chair
el sillín saddle (bicycle)
el sillón armchair
simpático (-a/-os/-as) nice, friendly
sin without
el sitio place
la situación situation
sobrar to have to spare
el sobre envelope
sobre on, upon, about
la sobrina niece

el sobrino nephew
el sofá sofa
el sol sun
solamente only
el soldado soldier
soler to be in the habit of
sólo only
el sombrero hat
sonar to sound, to ring
sonreír to smile
soñar to dream
la sopa soup
sorprender to surprise
la sortija ring
subir to go up, to bring up,
   to climb
el suelo ground, floor
la suerte luck
el supermercado supermarket

el tabaco tobacco
tal such
la talla size
también also
tampoco neither
tanto so much
tanto (-a/-os/-as) so much, so many
tardar to take time
tarde late
la tarde afternoon, evening
la (tarjeta) postal postcard
la taza cup
el té tea
el teatro theatre
el telegrama telegram
telefonear to phone, to ring up
el teléfono telephone
la televisión television
temprano early
tener to have
tener éxito to succeed
el tenis tennis
tercero (-a/-os/-as) third
terminar to finish
la terraza balcony, terrace
la tía aunt
el tiempo weather

la **tienda** shop
el **tío** uncle
tocar to touch, to play (an instrument)
todo everything
todo el mundo everybody
todos los días every day
tomar to take, to have (food, drink)
la **tónica** tonic water
tonto (-a/-os/-as) silly
la **tortilla** omelette
trabajar to work
el **trabajo** job, work
traducir to translate
traer to bring
tras after (behind)
tratar (de) to try
el **tren** train
el **tribunal** law court
triste sad
triunfar to succeed
el/la **turista** tourist
tronar to thunder

un (-a/-os/-as) a, one, some
la **universidad** university
único only (thing)
usar to use
útil useful
la **uva** grape

las **vacaciones** holidays
vacilar to hesitate
¡vale! all right!, OK!

valer to be worth
valer la pena to be worth it
varios (-as) several
la **velocidad** speed
vender to sell
venir to come
la **ventana** window
la **ventanilla** window (of car)
ver to see
el **verano** summer
la **verdad** truth
verdadero (-a/-os/-as) true
verde green
verse to see each other
el **vestido** dress
vestirse to get dressed
viajar to travel
el **viaje** journey
viejo (-a/-os/-as) old
el **viento** wind
el **viernes** Friday
el **vino** wine
el **violín** violin
visitar to visit
vivir to live
volver to return, to go back
la **voz** voice

ya already
ya no no longer

la **zapatería** shoe shop
el **zapato** shoe
la **zona** area

In this section, (v.) for verb is set against any English headword which might otherwise be read as a noun. The same goes for a few adjectives (a.). In the Spanish translations, an asterisk * indicates adjectives which change their form according to gender/number; the masculine singular (or, where appropriate, the masculine plural) is shown.

a un, una
about sobre
accept aceptar
accident accidente
accompany acompañar
according to según
accountant contable
accuse acusar
actor actor
actress actriz
address señas
advise aconsejar
aeroplane avión
after después (de)
after (= behind) tras
afternoon tarde
against contra
airport aeropuerto
allow dejar(se), permitir
all right! ¡vale!
almost casi
along por
a lot mucho*
already ya
also también
always siempre
amount cantidad
amusing divertido
announce anunciar
answer (v.) contestar
any alguno*
anything cualquier cosa
apartment piso
aperitif aperitivo
appear presentarse
apple manzana
approach (v.) acercarse

April abril
architect arquitecto
area zona
argue discutir
argument discusión
arm brazo
armchair sillón
arrest (v.) arrestar
arrive llegar
as como
ask preguntar
ask for pedir
assist asistir
at a
attend asistir
attend to ocuparse de
aunt tía
autumn otoño

badly mal
bag bolsa
bakery panadería
balcony terraza
ball pelota
bank banco
bath (v.) bañar
bathe (oneself) bañarse
bathroom baño
be ser, estar
be able poder
be missing faltar
be quiet callarse
beach playa
bed cama
bedroom dormitorio
beer cerveza
before ante, antes de

begin empezar
beginning (n.) principio
behind detrás (de)
believe creer
belong pertenecer
better mejor
between entre
bicycle bicicleta
big grande*
bill (= account) cuenta
birthday cumpleaños
biscuit galleta
bite (v.) morder
black negro*
blame culpa
blind (a.) ciego*
blue azul*
boat (= rowing) barca
boat (= ship) barco
book (v.) reservar
book libro
book-keeper contable
boot (of car) maletero
boring aburrido*
bother molestar
bottle botella
box caja
boy muchacho, niño
bracelet pulsera
brandy coñac
bread pan
bread roll panecillo
break romper, romperse
breakfast desayuno
bring traer
bring up subir
broken roto*
brother hermano
build construir
building edificio
bullet bala
burglar ladrón
bus autobús
bus stop parada de autobús
busy concurrido*, ocupado*
but pero
butcher's shop carnicería
buy comprar

call (v.) llamar
call oneself llamarse
cancel cancelar
capital capital
car automóvil, coche
car door portezuela
car park aparcamiento
carry llevar
cat gato
cathedral catedral
celebrate celebrar
censor (v.) censurar
certain cierto
chair silla
change cambio
charge (v.) cobrar
charming encantador*
cheap barato*
chemist's shop farmacia
cheque cheque
chocolates bombones
choose escoger
church iglesia
cigarette cigarrillo, pitillo
cinema cine
city ciudad
clever listo*
client cliente
climate clima
climb (v.) subir
clock reloj
close (v.) cerrar
clothes ropa
coach autocar
coast costa
coat abrigo
coffee café
coincidence casualidad
cold (a.) frío*
colleague compañero
colour color
come venir
come across
  encontrarse con
come in entrar
companion compañero
complain quejarse
computer ordenador

concert concierto
consent (v.) consentir
conservative conservador
contact contacto
content oneself contentarse
conversation conversación
cook (v.) guisar
correct correcto*
cost (v.) costar
count (v.) contar
countryside campo
cousin primo (m.), prima (f.)
covered cubierto*
cry (v.) llorar
cup taza
cupboard armario
curiosity curiosidad
custom (= habit) costumbre
Customs Aduana

damage daño
dance (v.) bailar
dance, dancing baile
dangerous peligroso*
date fecha
daughter hija
dawn (v.) amanecer
day día
day off día libre
dead muerto*
December diciembre
decide decidir(se)
delay retraso
delicious delicioso*
delighted encantado*
demonstration manifestación
depend depender
describe describir
desk escritorio
die morir, morirse
difficult difícil*
difficulty dificultad
diligently diligentemente
dine, have dinner cenar
dining room comedor
dinner cena
director director
disaster desastre

disc disco
dismiss despedir
do hacer
doctor médico
document documento
dog perro
door puerta
doubt (v.) dudar
doubtful dudoso*
drawer cajón
dream (v.) soñar
dress vestido
drink (v.) beber
drink, to have a d. tomar una copa
drink bebida, aperitivo
drive (v.) conducir
dry seco*
dry (v.) secar
dry oneself secarse
during durante
each cada
early temprano
earn ganar
easily fácilmente
easy fácil*
eat comer
edge borde
egg huevo
eighth octavo*
either ... or o ... o
elevator (= lift) ascensor
employee empleado
end fin
engine motor
English inglés*
enough bastante
enough, to be e. bastar
envelope sobre
error error
euro euro
evening tarde
everybody todo el mundo
every day todos los días
everything todo
expect esperar
expense gasto
expensive caro*
explanation explicación

factory fábrica
fairly bastante
fall in love enamorarse
famous famoso*
far lejos
fast rápido*
father padre
fault culpa
fax fax
February febrero
feel (v.) sentirse
few poco*
fifth quinto*
film película
find (v.) encontrar
find out enterarse
fine (a.) estupendo*
fine (= penalty) multa
finish (v.) acabar, terminar
fire, by the f. al fuego
first primero*
fish (as food) pescado
fish (animal) pez
fit in (v.) caber
flat (= apartment) piso
floor suelo, piso
flour harina
flower flor
fog niebla
follow seguir
food comida
foot pie
football pools quinielas
for para
forbid prohibir
forget olvidar(se)
forgive perdonar
free libre*
freeze (v.) helar
French francés*
frequently frecuentemente
fresh fresco*
Friday viernes
friend amigo (m.),
   amiga (f.)
friendly simpático*
from de, desde
full lleno*

funeral entierro
follow seguir
fourth cuarto*

garden jardín
generous espléndido*
gentleman señor
German alemán*
get angry enfadarse
get better mejorar
get dark anochecer
get dressed vestirse
get married casarse
get tired cansarse
get up levantarse
get wet mojarse
gin ginebra
girl muchacha, chica, niña
give dar
give back devolver
glad, to be g. alegrarse
glasses (= optical) gafas
glove guante
go ir
go away irse
go back volver
go down bajar
go for a walk dar un paseo
go on seguir
go on holiday ir de vacaciones
go out salir
go shopping ir de compras
go to bed acostarse
go to sleep dormirse
go up subir
gold oro
good bueno*
goodbye adiós
goodwill buena intención
grandfather abuelo
grape uva
grave (= serious) grave*
green verde*
greet saludar
ground (floor) suelo
habit costumbre
habit, to be in the h. of soler
half medio*

hand mano
handbag bolso
happen ocurrir
happy contento*, feliz*
hat sombrero
hate (v.) odiar
hate each other odiarse
have haber, tener
have (food/drink) tomar
have a good time divertirse
have left quedar
have a rest descansar
have to spare sobrar
hear oír
heat calor
hello hola
help (v.) ayudar
help each other ayudarse
helper ayudante
hesitate vacilar
hill colina
hire (v.) alquilar
history historia
hit (v.) pegar
holidays vacaciones
home casa
hope (v.) esperar
horrible horrible*
horse caballo
hospital hospital
hot caliente*
hotel hotel
hoarse ronco*
hour hora
house casa
how como
how much cuánto
hunger hambre
husband marido
hurry (v.) darse prisa

ice cream helado
idea idea
ill enfermo*
illustration ilustración
important importante*
in a, en
in front delante (de)

in that case entonces
inaugurate inaugurar
incredible increíble*
inherit heredar
injury daño, herida
insist insistir
instructions instrucciones
insult (v.) insultar
insurance company compañía
   de seguros
intelligent inteligente*
interest (v.) interesar
interesting interesante*
introduce presentar
invite invitar
Italian italiano*

jacket chaqueta
January enero
job trabajo
journey viaje
judge juez
July julio
June junio
just justo*
keep (v.) guardar
key llave
kilometre kilómetro
kind amable
kitchen cocina
know conocer, saber

lack (v.) faltar
lady señora
language idioma
last (= past) pasado*
last (v.) durar
late tarde
laugh (v.) reírse
law ley
law court tribunal
lay the table poner la mesa
lazy holgazán*
lean out asomarse
learn aprender
leave behind dejar
leg pierna
lend prestar

less menos
let (v.) dejar
letter carta
lift (= elevator) ascensor
light luz
like (v.) gustar
like como
line fila
listen escuchar
little pequeño*, poco*
little (= amount) poco
live (v.) vivir
living room salón
London Londres
long largo*
longer más tiempo
look (v.) mirar
look after cuidar
look for buscar
lose perder
lose one's way perderse
lorry camión
lounge salón
love (v.) querer
love each other quererse
lovely delicioso*
luck suerte
luggage equipaje
lunch comida
lunch time hora de comer

machine máquina
madam señora
magazine revista
mail correo
main principal*
make hacer
make an effort esforzarse
man hombre
manage conseguir
manager gerente
many muchos*
map mapa
March marzo
market mercado
married casado*
matches cerillas
matter (v.) importar

May mayo
meal comida
meat carne
meet (v.) encontrarse con
message recado
midnight medianoche
milk leche
minor leve*
miss (train etc) perder
Miss señorita
mist neblina
moment momento
Monday lunes
money dinero
month mes
more más
mother madre
motor motor
mountain montaña
move (v.) mover
Mr. señor
Mrs. señora
much mucho*
museum museo
music música
must deber

name nombre
near cerca
necklace collar
necktie corbata
need (v.) necesitar
neither tampoco
neither ... nor ni ... ni
nephew sobrino
never jamás, nunca
new nuevo*
news noticia
newspaper periódico
next próximo*
nice simpático*
niece sobrina
nightdress camisón
nobody nadie
noise ruido
no longer ya no
none ninguno*
no one nadie

north norte
note (= money) billete
nothing nada
notice (v.) fijarse en
novel novela
November noviembre
now ahora
nowadays hoy día
number número

obey obedecer
obtain conseguir
occupied ocupado*
October octubre
of de
of course claro
offer (v.) ofrecer
office despacho, oficina
often a menudo
OK vale
old viejo*
omelette tortilla
on sobre
one uno*
only solamente, sólo
only (thing) único
on top of encima
open (v.) abrir
opposite enfrente de
or o
orange naranja
order (v.) mandar, pedir
other otro*
owe deber

pack (v.) (suitcase) hacer la
  maleta
paint (v.) pintar
painter pintor
parcel paquete
parents padres
party fiesta
pass (v.) pasar
past pasado*
patience paciencia
pay (v.) pagar
peach melocotón
pen pluma

pencil lápiz
people gente
performance función,
  representación
perhaps acaso, quizás
person persona
petrol gasolina
photograph fotografía
piano piano
pick up (v.) recoger
picture cuadro
pill píldora
pity lástima
place (n.) lugar, sitio
play (theatre) obra (de teatro)
play (v.) jugar
play (an instrument) tocar
pleasant agradable*
pleased contento*
pleasure gusto
pocket bolsillo
police policía
policeman guardia, policía
poor pobre*
possibility posibilidad
post (= mail) correo
postcard (tarjeta) postal
postage stamp sello
practice práctica
prepare preparar
present (n.) regalo
president presidente
pretty bonito*
price precio
prize premio
problem problema
promise (v.) prometer
protestant protestante
provoke provocar
published publicado*
punish castigar
pupil alumno
purchases compras
put poner
put in meter
put on ponerse
quarter cuarto
queen reina

rain (v.) llover
read leer
ready dispuesto*
reason razón
reasonable razonable*
receive recibir
reduction rebaja
relatives parientes
remain quedar
remember acordarse (de), recordar
result resultado
return (v.) volver, devolver
rich rico*
ride a bike montar en bicicleta
right (= correct) correcto*
right (= direction) derecho*
ring (v.) (bell etc) sonar
ring (on finger) sortija, anillo
ring up telefonear
river río
road carretera
room cuarto, habitación
row (= line) fila
rowing boat barca
run away huir
Russian ruso*

sacrifice sacrificio
sad triste
saddle (on cycle) sillín
same mismo*
sandwich bocadillo
Saturday sábado
save (money) ahorrar
say (v.) decir
say goodbye despedirse
school escuela, colegio
sea mar
seafood marisco
season estación
seat asiento
second segundo*
see ver
see each other verse
seem parecer
seize apresar
sell vender
send enviar

September septiembre
serious grave*
serve servir
service servicio
seventh séptimo*
several varios*
severely severamente
shelf estante
sherry jerez
ship barco
shirt camisa
shoe zapato
shoe shop zapatería
shoot (v.) disparar
shop tienda
shop assistant dependiente, -a
shopping compras
shout (v.) gritar
show (v.) enseñar
shower ducha
sign (v.) firmar
silence silencio
silk seda
silly tonto*
sing cantar
sir señor
sister hermana
sit down sentarse
situation situación
sixth sexto*
size talla
sleep (v.) dormir, dormirse
slow lento*
slowly despacio
small pequeño*
smell (n.) olor
smile (v.) sonreír
smoke (v.) fumar
snow nieve
snow (v.) nevar
so así (que)
sofa sofá
so many tantos*
so much tanto, tanto*
soldier soldado
some unos, unas
some (= any) alguno*
somebody alguien

someone alguien
something algo
sour agrio*
son hijo
soon pronto
Spain España
sound (v.) sonar
soup sopa
speak hablar
speed velocidad
spend (time) pasar
sport deporte
spring (= season) primavera
start (a car) arrancar
station estación
stay (v.) quedarse
stop (v.) parar, pararse
straight directamente
strawberry fresa
street calle
strong fuerte*
student estudiante
study (v.) estudiar
stupid estúpido*
succeed tener éxito, triunfar
success éxito
such tal, semejante*
suffice bastar
sugar azúcar
suitcase maleta
summer verano
sun sol
Sunday domingo
supermarket supermercado
surprise (v.) sorprender
sweet dulce*
swimmer nadador
swimming pool piscina
table mesa
take tomar
take away llevarse, quitar
taken ocupado*
take off (clothes) quitarse
take time tardar
talk (v.) hablar
tall alto*
taste of saber a
tea té

teach enseñar
teacher profesor, -a
telegram telegrama
telephone teléfono
telephone (v.) telefonear
television televisión
tennis tenis
tenth décimo*
terrace terraza
test (v.) probar
thanks gracias
that ese*, que
that (= over there) aquel*
the el, los, la, las
theatre teatro
theft robo
then entonces
there allí
thief ladrón
thing cosa
third tercero*
thirst sed
this este*
these estos*
think pensar
those esos*
those (= over there) aquellos*
threaten amenazar
thunder (v.) tronar
Thursday jueves
thus así (que)
ticket billete
tie (= neck-) corbata
time hora
tired cansado*
to a
tobacco tabaco
today hoy
together juntos*
tomorrow mañana
too (much) demasiado
touch (v.) tocar
tourist turista
towards hacia
town ciudad
train tren
translate traducir
travel (v.) viajar

travel agent agencia de viajes
tree árbol
trouble (v.) molestar
trousers pantalones
true verdadero*
truth verdad
try probar, tratar (de)
try to intentar
Tuesday martes

ugly feo*
umbrella paraguas
unbearable insoportable*
uncle tío
under bajo
underneath debajo (de)
understand comprender
understand each other
  comprenderse
university universidad
until hasta
upon sobre
upstairs arriba
use (v.) usar
useful útil*
usually generalmente

very muy
village pueblo
violin violín
visit (v.) visitar
voice voz

wait (v.) esperar
waiter camarero
waken despertar
wake up despertarse
walk (v.) andar
want (v.) desear, querer
war guerra
wardrobe armario
warn avisar
warning (= sign) aviso

wash (v.) lavar
wash (oneself) lavarse
watch reloj
water agua
way (= road) camino
wear (v.) llevar
wealthy rico*
weather tiempo
wedding boda
Wednesday miércoles
week semana
well (= good) bien
what que
when cuando
where to adonde
which cual, que
while mientras
white blanco*
who que, quien, ¿quién?
whom quien, ¿quién?
wife mujer
willpower fuerza de
  voluntad
win (v.) ganar
wind viento
window ventana
window (of car) ventanilla
wine vino
winter invierno
wish (v.) desear
with con
without sin
wonderfully maravillosamente
word palabra
work (v.) trabajar
work trabajo
worry (v.) preocuparse
worth (to be w.) valer
worse peor
write escribir

year año
young joven*

Index

The numbers refer to section headings, not pages.